Payne Hollow Journal

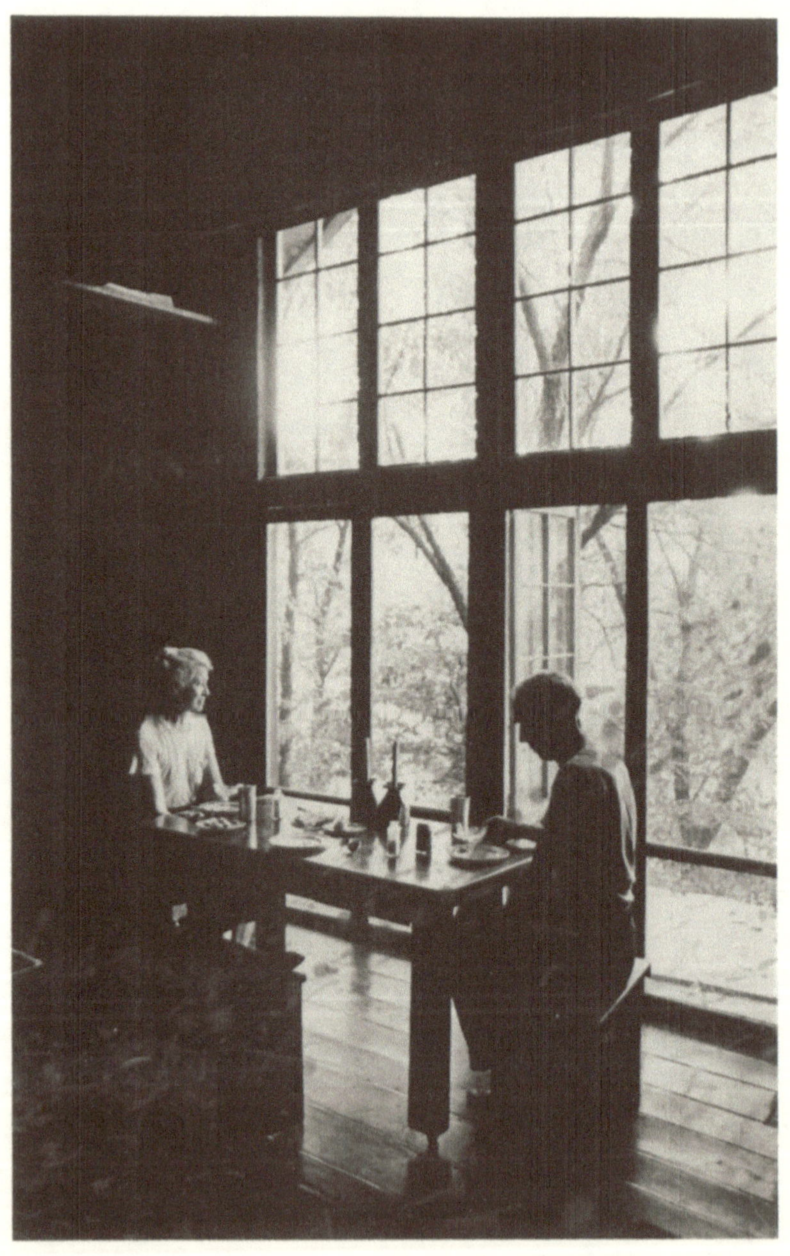

Payne Hollow Journal

Harlan Hubbard

WITH ILLUSTRATIONS BY THE AUTHOR

DON WALLIS, EDITOR

THE UNIVERSITY PRESS OF KENTUCKY

Illustration on page 97 courtesy of Florence Fowler Burdine; other woodcuts by Harlan Hubbard are reproduced courtesy of Claude W. Caddell.

Frontispiece: Harlan and Anna Hubbard at Payne Hollow. Photo by Bill Strode.

Paperback edition 2009

The University Press of Kentucky
Scholarly publisher for the Commonwealth,
serving Bellarmine University, Berea College, Centre College of Kentucky, Eastern Kentucky University, The Filson Historical Society, Georgetown College, Kentucky Historical Society, Kentucky State University, Morehead State University, Murray State University, Northern Kentucky University, Transylvania University, University of Kentucky, University of Louisville, and Western Kentucky University.

Editorial and Sales Offices: The University Press of Kentucky
663 South Limestone Street, Lexington, Kentucky 40508-4008
www.kentuckypress.com

Cataloging-in-Publication Data is available from the Library of Congress.

ISBN 978-0-8131-9325-0 (pbk: acid-free paper)

This book is printed on acid-free recycled paper meeting the requirements of the American National Standard for Permanence in Paper for Printed Library Materials.

Manufactured in the United States of America.

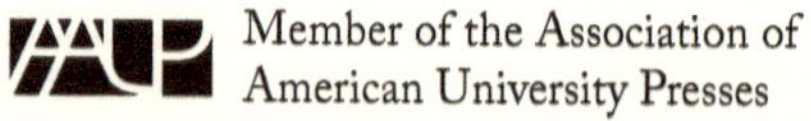

Member of the Association of American University Presses

Contents

Editor's Preface

Harlan Hubbard's *Payne Hollow Journal* is presented here not in conventional journal form—day by day, year by year—but season by season, to reflect the essential way the Hubbards lived: "All our living is regulated by the revolving seasons," Harlan wrote. "They determine what we do, what we think and talk about, what we eat, the pattern of each day."

The pattern of each day: the pattern of the seasons: the pattern of a life. Moving through the natural cycle of the seasons, the Hubbards' life at Payne Hollow was always changing, yet always the same; Harlan's appreciations were constant, and, like the seasons, constantly recurring and renewed, season after season, year after year. This is one of the wonders of life at Payne Hollow, and this presentation of Harlan's *Journal* honors it.

Harlan kept the *Journal* from 1952 through 1968; the year of each entry is noted in the text. Editing of the entries excludes the customary ellipses denoting deletions. Interested readers may consult the entire unedited journal at the University Archives of the University of Louisville, where many Hubbard materials are collected.

In editing Harlan's *Payne Hollow Journal,* I have sought to reflect the spirit in which he kept it: "I am deeply concerned with how each day, each minute is spent," Harlan wrote, "and this is a kind of memorial to the passing days."

Don Wallis

Introduction

Payne Hollow Journal is the third and final volume of the journals of Harlan Hubbard, artist, author, and wilderness homesteader whose life (1900–1988) is an enduring legend along the Ohio River. His journals tell the story of his life. In the first volume, *Journals 1929–1944,* Harlan grows into middle age a lonely, restless, often despairing seeker of his life's purpose and meaning. In the second volume, *Shantyboat Journal* (1944–1951), his life is transformed. He is no longer lonely—he has married a remarkable and gifted woman, Anna Wonder Eikenhout—and he is no longer restless or despairing: on the river he has found his place, and he has found purpose and meaning in his life.

> I had no theories to prove. I merely wanted to try living by my own hands, independent as far as possible from a system of division of labor in which the participant loses most of the pleasure of making and growing things for himself. I wanted to grow my own food, catch it in the river, or forage after it. In short, I wanted to do as much as I could for myself, because I had already realized from partial experience the inexpressible joy of so doing.

For seven years the Hubbards made their home on the river, living on the small houseboat (or "shantyboat") that Harlan built, at first as members of a shantyboat community near Cincinnati, then, for nearly five years, drifting down the Ohio and the Mississippi and in the bayous of Louisiana. They lived what Harlan called "a river way of life." For their food they caught fish in the river, grew gardens on the riverbank, and foraged in the woods; in their boat's cookstove and fireplace, they burned the wood Harlan cut and gathered on the shore; and they created together on board their tiny boat a household abundant with fulfilling work, purposeful leisure, art, music, fellowship, and love.

At the end of their long drifting journey, the Hubbards extended their "river way of life" onto the land. In the summer of 1952 they returned to the Ohio River and settled in a remote, secluded, abandoned place—Payne Hollow—nestled in the hills on the Kentucky shore. Here they built a house and established a homestead, and they lived at Payne Hollow for the rest of their lives, until Anna's death, at age 83, in 1986, and Harlan's death, at 88, two years later. *Payne Hollow Journal* is Harlan's testament to the place and the life they lived there.

The Hubbards settled at Payne Hollow because, Harlan wrote: "We were both led on by a common desire to get down to earth and express ourselves by creating a setting for our life together which would be in harmony with the landscape." They began with the building of their house, a simple cabin the same small size as their houseboat, overlooking the river, "peering out from the trees, so firmly planted in the hillside that it seems to have grown there," Harlan wrote. "The long roof lines continue the slope with an upward thrust and a window, tall and wide, reflects the blue sky."

In harmony with the landscape, yes; and the Hubbards lived their lives in harmony with the seasons, their lives changing as the seasons changed, and as the landscape changed with the seasons:

Winter is their freest, purest season, when the Payne Hollow landscape is spare and silent, except for the ringing sounds of birds singing—and the ringing sound of Harlan's axe. In winter Harlan enacts the ceremony of the cutting of wood, venturing out even in the harshest of weather to do his pleasurable work: "The day cold and bright, the earth frozen all day. . . . It is a joy to cut wood on the snowy slopes." In the winter evenings Harlan and Anna sit together by the fireplace and read to each other, or play music together, or quietly perform their household tasks. "Winter," Harlan wrote, "an enduring time, when change almost comes to a stand."

In early spring the landscape is reborn, suddenly and dramatically: "The simple design of winter is shattered and replaced by a complexity which is almost chaos." Now "the earth is vibrant with life. All our senses are caressed." Soon the season settles: "The softness and gentleness of spring, the subdued colors glowing in the rain. . . ." The rain nourishes the earth, and the Hubbards enact the ceremony of the garden. Gardening, Harlan wrote, "is the keystone of our living here," the source of food and "rich rewards to the spirit as well." Harlan and Anna spend long springtime days planting new gardens and renewing their old gardens, and they gather wild plants in the flourishing woods. It is a busy, productive, exciting time; Harlan writes of the "exultation" of spring.

Summer is a season of release. The joyful intensity the Hubbards feel in spring is relaxed in summer. After its springtime flowering the earth now seems to be at rest; the river lies still in its summer bed. Gardening becomes less urgent. Harlan falls asleep in the shade of a summer afternoon: "When I awoke it was to a new existence. I seemed to have infinite time and could do as I pleased." His spirit enacts a rising affirmation: "Surely joy, like health, is a natural condition for living."

Autumn is for Harlan "the blossoming of the year," stunning in its beauty; in their new autumn colors "the river hills are glorious." The season is transcendent: "The ripening of the earth, from the green summer to the varied and brilliant colors of autumn, affords a glimpse of life on a higher plane than we know. It is marvelous that our daily lives go on amid this splendor. . . . I wonder and enjoy as I go through the day." The Hubbards complete the harvest of their gardens, storing their food in the cellar for winter: "One feels truly wealthy. . . . The cellar now gives one a feeling of richness and security, an abundance laid up against the coming time of cold."

As autumn's glory fades from the landscape, inside the Hubbards' house "a new season has begun. . . . To sit by a fire, to burn candles, such are the delights of the new season. . . . One feels that he stands at the entrance to some grand new region, where all is new and changing." Soon the blessed season of winter will be renewed, and with it Harlan's most cherished work: "The fire in the fireplace brings woodcutting to mind."

Then it is truly winter again, Harlan's deepest-lived season: "I rejoice in the winter landscape." "How great a revelation it is!"

In all seasons Harlan fishes in the river, tends his herd of goats on the hillside, and maintains his homestead with constant, skillful work. And in all seasons he is an artist. In his workshop he sustains his life's work as an artist, painting pictures of the river and the hills and the Payne Hollow landscape, joining together his life and his art: "Just a little solid creative painting, and the day is good. It brings us closer to the earth, makes the present moment exhilarating, the future hopeful." "Painting is the element without which my life is not complete." "It brings everything into balance and harmony."

These are, briefly sketched, the Seasons of Payne Hollow. They form, along with Payne Hollow itself—their place on earth—the essential context and content of the life the Hubbards lived there, a life so "exquisitely and deeply civilized," Wendell Berry has written, that it is "one of the finest accomplishments of our time."

I said the life of the Hubbards is an Ohio River legend. I knew of it as a child, growing up on the river at Madison, on the Indiana shore around a long sweeping bend upriver from Payne Hollow. Everyone in Madison knew of the Hubbards. We all talked and wondered about these extraordinary people, so different from anyone else we knew. This was their legend:

He was an artist and she was a musician, and together they left their worldly lives behind them, to drift down the river all the way to the sea. Then they came back, to live forever in a wilderness place, remote from civilization, *apart from the world.* They built their own home and grew their own food; they lived off the river and the land. They had no electricity and they paid no bills. They never needed to go to the store. "They live primitive lives," people said, "like the old pioneers used to live"—except that in their rustic cabin in the woods the man wrote books and painted pictures, and the woman played her grand piano. They were the Hubbards of Payne Hollow, a place you could get to only by crossing the river in a boat, unless you walked a mile down a steep rugged hill, the only other way to get there. Payne Hollow was not far away from Madison, but—*apart from the world*: this was the essence of the legend of the Hubbards. In town we were forever curious about them. They lived a life we could not understand, and yet somehow admired and were drawn to, in some deep longing way alive to the truth of it.

What *is* the truth of it? What is the meaning of Payne Hollow? No one I knew growing up could answer this question, or even ask it, but I believe it was, in some vague and unacknowledged sense, on everyone's mind. It remained on my mind as I grew up and went away from the river, and it was still on my mind when I came back. (Always you come back to the river.) As a child I had been to Payne Hollow, and as a man I went back to Payne Hollow, and I was welcomed by the Hubbards, at first as a visitor, later as a friend; and I went back to Payne Hollow again and again, to experience some of the finest moments of my life.

At Payne Hollow the Hubbards lived as they truly wished to live, in a natural accord with the earth, accepting nature's gifts of elemental pleasures: sunlight and breeze, wind sounds and bird songs, hard good work. Always their work was their pleasure. Anna gave praise to "the precious daylight hours," for they gave her light to work by. She was an elegant woman, tall, fair, feminine, and beautiful. She moved through her days with an effortless grace. In a corner of the Hubbards' small house was a grand piano Anna played in the evenings with the skill and measured passion of an accomplished musician, which she was. She played by candlelight. The Hubbards' house possessed such a natural refinement that Anna's grand piano, stately and ornate, seemed to belong there, as naturally as did the rough timbers and boards and the smooth stone of the hearth.

The house seemed to have shaped itself to the Payne Hollow landscape, crowning a rounded knoll on the hollow's hillside, extending the rise of the earth; and Harlan said Yes, this was true in a sense, for in building the house he had planned no design, had just let it take its own shape. Yet it was purely Harlan's house. As Anna said, "No one but an artist could have built it. No one in the world but Harlan could have built this house." He had made no plan, Harlan said, but when an artist makes a house it will form itself to his vision, the way his art must do. This is what I came to know about Harlan Hubbard, that in everything he did, in all the motions of his living, he enacted his essential self.

I would help him cut wood, though I was of little help: such pleasure he took in it, mostly I just stood and watched him: raw-boned, lean, his leathered skin taut on his muscled bones. When he paused to rest in the rhythm of his work, he stood on the earth rooted to it like a tree. His face was bright and new as a child's.

Sometimes we would eat a noonday dinner, a ceremony in the Payne Hollow day. It was in summer the first time I experienced this event. Anna served us broiled catfish, which Harlan had caught that morning in the river, and a lavish salad from their garden, tomatoes and comfrey and wild, vivid mint; our dessert was rhubarb glistened with elderberries, which Anna had gathered that morning in the woods. She served the food on china hand-painted blue. We sat at a walnut table Harlan had fashioned out of driftwood, by a wall full of windows open to the sky. We were bathed in the sun's soft light. Birds sang. There was a tingling breeze dancing through the hollow, playing in the leaves of the trees. I gazed out at the river in the distance, searching for some words to say, but found none. I thought of what people in Madison said, that the Hubbards lived a primitive life. I heard myself murmur, "You have all the advantages"—and was embarrassed by this; but Harlan and Anna graciously accepted my praise, knowing what I meant.

Harlan Hubbard had a wild, wild soul. That was his essential self. Everything—his art, his writing, all his *work*, his way of life—flowed from this source. By wild I mean fresh, bright, gentle, subtle, alert, beautiful, and free. Harlan had the soul of a shy wild bird, of a wildflower growing in the woods, of the leaves of a tree blowing softly in the wind. I also mean alone, self-contained, apart from the world. Harlan wrote in his book *Payne Hollow:*

> I yearn for the wild, I lean toward its absolute solitude. . . . Today as I swam in the river I looked up with a wild duck's eye into the trees waving as the wind rushed through them, lightly rattling the cottonwood leaves. . . . Suddenly, I felt alone on the earth, as I do when lying on the damp ground in spring to see closely the bloodroot raising its leaf sheath through the mold. These moments are not rare. I can summon them when I feel the need to retire into the wilderness. For this is my wilderness, untouched by man, of infinite grace and harmony.

Many times with the Hubbards I experienced moments—fleeting moments—of infinite grace and harmony; but still I do not have an answer to my question: What is the meaning of Payne Hollow? *Happiness* is the meager best I can do. Harlan and Anna were happy at Payne Hollow: this is the meaning of their lives. I do not mean that they were *simply* "happy," free of care or worry or conflict, or even at times of despair; I do mean truly and profoundly happy, deeply contented, truly self-rewarded and profoundly fulfilled.

Yet this remains an insufficient, merely sentimental answer unless it can be considered within a cultural context of the meaning of most people's lives. Harlan well knew the truth of his mentor Thoreau's sad observation that most men live lives of quiet desperation. Harlan knew this but could not understand it: The "radiant beauty" of the earth, Harlan wrote, "should be an unending source of wonder and joy, yet most people live and die without noticing it." *His* truth was: "There is no need to live a life of fear and apprehension. Happiness is a natural condition, and faith is the foundation of all." His faith was fully placed in the "gentle, soft-edged creation which is wild nature, ever cheerful and friendly, a solace to the spirit of man." This is why in his *Payne Hollow Journal* Harlan's celebrations of the sky, the snow, the sunrise and moonrise, the river and the earth are all so heartfelt and full of meaning. In this "wild nature" Harlan's soul *lived:* at Payne Hollow "I rejoiced that I could live so completely in nature."

And so life at Payne Hollow embraced at its daily core everything the Hubbards needed and wanted; and they sacrificed nothing to gain it, not even all the time they spent doing all their hard and constant work, for in the deepest sense they loved to do it: their work was at once the source and the substance, the very enactment of their happiness. Harlan wrote in his journal:

> To arise in the frosty morning at the point of daybreak, climb the hill and cut wood, while the sky lightens above the soaring trees; to eat this wholesome, sweet food; to use my body, hands and mind at the endless work I have to do; to read by the firelight, to sleep warm and snug; all this shared and enjoyed by my loving partner—what manner of a man originated this idea of a happier life beyond death?

Anna, nearing the end of her life, asked by a friend if she looked forward to being in Heaven, smiled and said she was already there: "Heaven is Payne Hollow."

Wendell Berry understands another meaning of Payne Hollow. He knew the Hubbards well, and, as he wrote, "One cannot know of Harlan and Anna's life without rejoicing in it and in the good human possibilities it represents." Their life at Payne Hollow was "exceptionally authentic, coherent, and attractive," a way of life that "reunites mind and body and spirit, and so makes of a man or woman a whole being." This is what I mean by happiness; Wendell Berry suggests a broader meaning. The Hubbards' life at Payne Hollow, he wrote, was "not a life merely personal in its significance; it was an exemplary way of living in America." It is a way of living that is necessarily the way of the future, not only because it transcended the human self-divisions of the present "modern world"—the crippling divisions of mind and body and spirit—but because it was lived so well in the kind of way and the kind of place that human beings must learn to live in.

Harlan Hubbard "set himself against the 'modern world,'" Wendell Berry wrote, "in order to live in the world itself, the natural and immemorial world, as fully and joyfully as possible. . . . He lived at the crossways of a vital paradox: by having little, he had much; by living frugally, he lived abundantly; by living 'apart from the world,' he lived in the world intimately and truly." This is the example he set, for others to follow. Wendell Berry, contemplating Harlan's life, found—another vital paradox—that "it became possible for me to imagine that Harlan, who lived so conscientiously apart from what most people consider the history of the modern world, will at last enter that history as a significant part of it and have an influence upon it." The life of the Hubbards at Payne Hollow is of "paramount historical significance," he wrote, because "they lived and thrived in a place in which, by the conventional assumptions of our time, all human possibilities were exhausted. . . . The place was available to the Hubbards because no one else saw any good in it."

> Such a life can be dismissed as inconsequential only by those who refuse to see the overriding irony of our present economic life: that "growth" is inescapably shrinking us. We are living within ever-widening margins of abandoned or abused or despised or ruined land—the "fringes" of our society, which our children will have to inhabit and make the best of, if they can. They must either make the best of them as Harlan and Anna did—by poverty of means, by great skill, by love—or endure them at their worst.

The Hubbards' life at Payne Hollow, then, points to the path future generations may take toward the salvation of their world.

Don Wallis

Spring

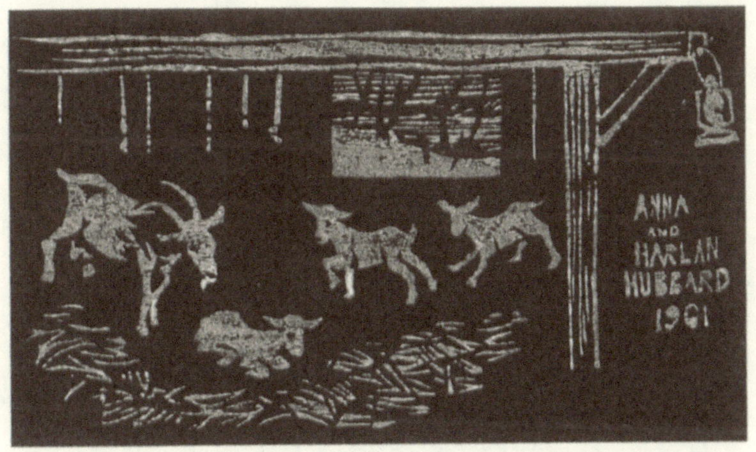

March

March 1 When we are away from Payne Hollow, that place does not seem real or possible; when we consider even living here in the way we do, that seems a mistaken gesture; yet on our return here all comes into its proper place and perspective, and the rest of the world is feverish and unbalanced. It is hard to explain our situation, to give reasons for our living this way to people who have no understanding or sympathy. Unless they have had some experience or yearning in this direction, they cannot even imagine our life here could be a success. The key to it all is a love of nature, I think. I want to live on the earth, which cannot be done in the city or any of its extensions. It is not enough merely to go into the country for an hour, a day, week or season. I want to feel a touch of the wildness in the minutest acts. It must be like the air itself. *1955*

March 2 Snow fell steadily during the windless night. The earth was radiant when we could see, even though the sun did not shine. A still day, an even light all through. To match the snow, I changed my routine, making an easel of driftwood and painting at the first picture since last summer. Now all other preoccupations take their rightful place, and I am released from all sense of duty toward them. *1953*

In the late afternoon, when the day first begins to shade into evening, I row across the still river. . . . Rowing, I have a fine chance to view the snowy hillside. Much is revealed by the snow—the height and extent of the cliffs, the number of cedars, and particularly the outline of the hill, which is firm white against the dark mass of trees. When the forest floor is dark colored it gradually fades into the trees on top. The faintest colors stand out against the white background—the warmth of budding maples and elms, even a flush of green on the weeping willow. *1953*

I gather some groundnuts left bare by the falling water. We have some for supper, and enjoy their sweet, earthy taste. *1953*

A feature of today was a flock of robins on the snow near the cabin. How warm their color against the white. Later I saw a large flock in the air. Perhaps it covered an acre. The resident birds were especially lively this morning. Perhaps the snow inspires them. Continued songs from titmice, cardinals, song sparrows, and wrens. That is our choir here these days. A passing bluebird or goldfinch warbles now and then, the crows call, and whirring woodpeckers are heard. *1953*

River still rising, swift current, drift, in islands and scattered, some big logs and chunks. I watch all through the day the steady flow, sucking through the trees. *1955*

Anna reported what she had heard about the man in space. It is typical of this age—a costly undertaking directed by the government, the individual submerged in numbers. And it has no contact with reality. It all takes place in the minds of people. *1966*

The morning was perfectly clear, and cold. The flooded river shows its character even by starlight. One hears the ruffle of the current as it swerves into the trees, and the distant hills are lower, even in the dim light. *1962*

This day might be called spring-like, by ordinary standards, quite mild it is. Good to step outside without protecting myself from cold. The sun shines warm and pale. I feel its influence. Perhaps the winter of my discontent is gone. Even heard a phoebe singing near the house. *1966*

March 3 Cool and cloudy, wind NW, river rising. Yesterday a visit from Carl Turner who lives on the River Road below Plowhandle Point. A river man, who can tell all about the local packet trade, or the last 50 years of it. Also, he bought the johnboat which I caught in the last rise. Upon his insistence, I priced it at ten dollars, which I thought very low. He said he didn't believe he could make out for more than seven, to which I agreed. He had but six with him, and I accepted 2 bales of poor quality alfalfa hay, which he left at the landing when he came down for the johnboat. . . . *1958*

March 4 Yesterday was a rough day. A strong south wind, warm and rainy, made a rough river of it. . . . The johnboat, which I had pulled out the night before, came afloat and was tossed by the waves. What a rolling we would have had, if afloat. The waves break on the submerged bar, and send in large swells against the bank. The shore above the creek is being scoured away, and trees undermined, by current and waves. Below the creek is a sandy shore apparently building out. . . . It was a cold wind this morning, at times very dark, with snow. The afternoon cleared and tonight all the stars shine. It is exciting to look down on the river, where patches of drift skirt the shore, driven to this side by the wind. The water is muddy. *1953*

I worked in the garden, chopping ground for potatoes. Again the feel and smell of fresh earth, the green grass, flowering elms and maples, bird song, the rushing muddy river. Perhaps I do not feel it so deeply as I once did, or I would be painting; but that will come again. The ecstasy may not be so keen, but it is there, inward. That is what I live by, still, and always. *1955*

A rainy evening. I hear the creek running over stones, back up the hollow, beyond the backwater. . . . River still rising, slowly. On a dark, rainy night, one feels that it may rise fast, to unheard-of high levels. In the sunny afternoon it seems to be at the crest. *1955*

It is exciting now to see the tawny water of the river and the clear green water of the creek meeting, but not mingling. I have never noticed the creek water to be so green, and it is in sharp contrast with the russet field and hillside. *1961*

The high water is such an unusual circumstance that it forces itself on our consciousness always, yet being natural and not extreme, it can be enjoyed. *1962*

I was busy all morning at different chores, but the afternoon as usual was one of rest and silence. Why not make every afternoon like this? Try it for a week. I will, when I get caught up with the current work. *1962*

The rain is relaxing, you conclude that not so much is expected of you, after all. *1963*

March 5 A definite entrance of spring. The day turned quite warm, with a strong south wind which rolled up waves on the muddy river. Heard a phoebe. The first planting, and the first fishing.

The afternoon of this rainy day we went to Hanover College dressed in our best clothes, under rain clothes, to receive whoever of our friends or other interested people who might also go there to see my paintings. Perhaps 50 were there, at a random guess, and we both talked to each one. Some were our farm friends from Trimble County, some Hanover faculty people, some from Madison and Louisville. I felt depressed about the affair, but did get many responses to the pictures, nearly every one of the 32 was mentioned as a favorite which seems to be the accepted way of judging. What right have they to pick out one or two as "better"? I think that after all, few people have a true feeling for graphic art, as with music. Most judge solely from the pictorial side. Yet who can say that they are not influenced by the plastic form, unknown to themselves?

It is warm, a thick fog hangs over the river, gentle rain—high water weather. *1963*

March 6 The snow was reflected, the white shores, whitened trees, and snow or drift against the dark water. . . . How little snow it takes to transform the world. That is the glory of winter. *1962*

Whatever may come, I cannot complain of the service my body has rendered, if such a complaint were possible, such a separation between me and my body. At any rate, I have seldom or never been prevented or even hindered from doing what I decided from physical weakness. *1962*

This was a fine March day, wind, white clouds, sunshine; also, high water and full creeks. Yesterday we heard the phoebe about the yard, its sharp meager song expressing perfectly this particular season, with its winter barrenness and faint promise of spring. *1963*

March 7 River seems at a stand (23 feet). . . . It is always novel and exciting to see the water so close to the house. It is alive. *1964*

The current this rise seems remarkably strong for the Ohio. Bill [Shadrick]'s cabin is on dry, or rather very wet and muddy land now, and Bill was inside shovelling out the wet mud—1½ inches on his floor, he said. . . . Bill had a hard day today or at least half a day, getting up early to get down to the river bank, dragging his johnboat into deep water, unloading the float so that the stuff could be packed up the hill later, cleaning out the mud—all heavy work. He was exhausted and shaky. It is too much for him, but he does well to go on with it, even though it kills him. What would be gained by sparing himself, going to a doctor, avoiding all exertion? He has the satisfaction of taking care of himself, and living in the place and manner he desires.* *1962*

March 8 Whenever I return from the society of people, I feel that I have talked too much, rather said some unconsidered words, and not come up to the mark when I should; that I have given the wrong impression of myself and my thoughts. I mean well, have a true love for my friends, admire their virtues, and see some of their faults and weaknesses. I am not a congenial person. I know of no one who likes me unreservedly. My friends feel that I am critical of them and of the way they live. They have a suspicion, or in some cases a definite opinion, that I am something of an imposter. Yet our meeting and conversation is

---

**June 17* This morning we attended the funeral of Bill Shadrick, who died in the hospital at Madison on June 15, shortly after we had seen and talked with him. There was peace and dignity about the service, but I could not connect Bill with it. . . . It cannot be said that we were intimate with Bill, but he is woven into our life here and we will miss him in many ways. I admire his life, he achieved a rare simplicity. He was a more successful philosopher than most and he quitted life cleanly, leaving no estate that anyone would quarrel over, for who would want his leaky johnboat and old nets? He did not suffer, and was no trouble to anyone. He would have preferred an instant death on the riverbank, but three weeks in the hospital were not bad. *1962*

stimulating on both sides and I am accorded an admiration and approval which is often conditional and grudged. *1954*

Yesterday I saw green shadows on the snow—a pale blue green, a sea green. The sunlight, shining in almost a level line, tinged the snow with pink. Then this morning, when all was frozen hard, the quiet song of a dove came from far up on the hill. *1960*

Yesterday evening the new moon shone over the western horizon, and when night came on the sky was full of stars. *1962*

Probably this experiment of living here will be regarded as a failure in the end, perhaps even by Anna; but to me, it will not be a failure. I knew in the beginning it could not be an obvious and complete success. *1962*

The sun rises and sets, it is day and night, it will go on thus for a long time. You get to think you are part of it and your circumstances are related to the cosmos, but one day your little system will break down and the day and night will rotate indifferently. Can this be? It seems more like the sunrise and sunset, the moon and stars, this new season, they are part of me. I am sure they will never be the same without me, for no one could see them just as I do. *1963*

March 9 I would be unhappy and frustrated, living with college people, with intellectuals as friends and neighbors exclusively. I need the touch of earth in my society. That is why we enjoy our farm friends and neighbors. They are the sanest people, they keep society strong and healthy. If I made a picture, or wrote something, which they could not enjoy, I would be doubtful of its value in any sense. I do not expect them to understand or appreciate fully what I do, or try to do. Yet they come as near to understanding and appreciation as the intellectuals do. I think that the intellectuals have been duped by charlatans, by extremists whose work is as untruthful as the mental fodder of ordinary folk. *1954*

This high water is good for us. It puts the river in its proper place, and will carry us through much low water. It brings us closer to our shantyboat days. *1955*

Some painters, those called amateurs, express their enthusiasm and eagerness, their joy in painting, but with me it does not come so easily. Painting can only be done in some state of exaltation. It is a force that breaks through the routine of life, that transcends life itself, not one of life's pastimes. *1961*

River very swift and bankfull, but not much driftwood. No doubt we are in for the highest water since our coming here. *1964*

March 10 This evening the setting sun was streaming directly into the hollow, which was lighted from the river clear back to the barn. This happens only now, when the sun is just south of west, and when the trees are bare. I notice the buckeye buds are swelling, some nearly ready to open. Tiny white flowers are in bloom, and some blue ones no larger, all on the mossy plant that has as many variations as the fields. *1956*

I am moved by the dark hills, the bare, interlacing trees over the swift murky water, the rich warm color of the willow grove across the creek. *1963*

In the sunny afternoon we walked together out my wheelbarrow path and I showed Anna the trees I had cut during the winter for firewood. *1963*

March 11 Rain this morning, rain on high water, and one thinks of a flood that would rise higher than any ever known. *1963*

The frogs were croaking in Lee's Bottom this rainy day, and now I hear the concerted jingle of peepers from across the river downstream. As we rowed up the backwater we noticed the swelling buds of the soft maple and elm. A new note of color has been added to the landscape. This harmony that I have known for so long—the sharp, chill air, the bare, blue hills, the rich, subdued colors of the budding trees, the swirling, muddy water, the sound of peepers—it is elemental, everlasting. *1963*

River still rising, but slower, 37½ feet now, a rise of 3½ feet the past 24 hours. We crossed over this morning. . . . F. O'Neal was moving out of his house, on the lower floor, and there was all the excitement of rising water. *1964*

March 12 The river began to fall yesterday, slowly, but with no pause at the crest. This morning down a few inches, but the backwater looks different. One feels different, too. There is always a dread about rising water, it may go on up to unheard of levels. It is perhaps an instinctive, inherited fear of flood. As soon as the river begins to fall, however, even though it was doing no harm, there is a feeling of relief, relaxation; a sunny, cheerful outlook. *1955*

I paint a little along with much else. Painting lives its own life, independent of all. *1961*

Light intermittent rain the afternoon and evening. We enjoy an indoor afternoon together—a short nap, much playing, some reading (Heine). In this life our attainments fall far short of our desires, even of our capabilities. Yet the joy of a few quiet hours, the sympathy with the outlook and emotions of another (Bach), so close to us over the span of years, the background of the river and hills on this dark wet day—more than a background, it is the foundation, the main theme of my life—the contemplation of it, the resigned waiting, the quiet ecstasy. *1961*

I am all alive now, regenerated, re-constituted. Have made two watercolors. *1962*

One almost wishes that the change of seasons could stop at this point. For a brief period, perhaps 2 or 3 days when the river is at the crest of its rise, and is rising or falling almost imperceptibly, we have the feeling of a small lake in the backwater, where no current flows and the hillside across the creek rising from the water might be the opposite shore. The illusion is interfered with by the trees standing in the water, but even so it is a possible one, which is destroyed by the swift rising or falling of the water. Another day and the water will recede so quickly that all feeling of stability and permanence is lost. These are qualities that a river does not possess. *1963*

Anna baked some of her best bread today. *1965*

March 13 Buckeye buds opening on saplings. Bloodroot and the common white flower in bloom. The first catfish, 3 lb., caught in the backwater on a hook baited with a worm. River falling fast. *1955*

A mild, showery day, some hard rain, even a brief storm, and much blue sky. This evening clear, wind from NW and cooler. I dig parsnips for us and for the goats, some nearly every day, and wash them in the clear flowing creek. This is a rite of earliest spring, celebrating the cold clean water, the bare earth and the bare trees through which the sunshine passes freely. *1961*

March 14 The cold weather continues, the nights clear and sharp, mornings foggy, especially yesterday, when all the twigs and grass were white with frost. A fine sight when the sun was breaking through the shifting veils of fog. *1960*

The ground being too wet to "stir," I putter around in the "yard." Much in this line could be done, smoothing, polishing the hillside, but we like the unkempt wildness better. One must be wary of improvement. *1961*

I feel the faint hints of a return to painting. It begins by seeing as a painter, seeing pictures. This is a great happiness, and I still hope to paint something good, on a higher plane with some new elements. *1962*

River falls slowly, paths emerge. *1964*

March 15 P-coon, Farny's kid born Saturday, is fed by hand, by me, now five times a day; but this number will soon be reduced. All the duties with the goats I accept without question, without asking, "Does it pay?" The goats are part of our living here, not quite as "family" as the dogs, but of that order. *1961*

The great event of this day was the launching of our rebuilt canoe. I am delighted with it, its lightness and stability, just in its being a canoe. . . . Anna and I paddled about in the afternoon. *1964*

March 16 By invitation called at the Milton School, visited 1st, 2nd, 4th, 5th and 6th grades, showed 2 of my paintings, Bayou Chene and Corn Creek, and talked as best I could. Much impressed with the pupils, pleased with their interest and intelligent responses. The teachers are good—they like their work and the children, and I admired them greatly. Perhaps there is no need to worry about education—the mother-instinct will take care of it. *1956*

I feel uneasy and out-of-place, everywhere. I do not take to city ways, and am awkward and bungling. I cannot accept it at all. Others may drive to town and hear a concert, thinking nothing about it; but I am always conscious of the racing automobiles, wondering if the trip is worth the danger, risk and wear. I feel each piston stroke. *1956*

On Wed. morning, I walked up the hill to meet W. Powell and go to a sale on Liberty Road. A raw cold day. It would be more decent to burn the accumulation of a lifetime instead of dispersing it. How penurious is the human race. I was glad to escape from the sale before it commenced. *1956*

Every day we enjoy a salad of greens—dandelions, squaw corn, white top, narrow dock and the wild greens, with parsley, kale and rape from the garden. On top is a sprinkling of toasted sunflower seeds. Every other day, parsnips. *1961*

All good art is done with surety. No experimentation, no uncertainty as to form or procedure. Like a good craftsman, a good artist knows what he is doing. *1961*

Rain all day beginning soon after daybreak, not steady, but off and on, now pouring down, now drizzling, with and without thunder and lightning. The river, which had fallen perhaps two feet, started up again. The creek ran out, its freshly muddy water contrasting with the dark grayish color of the river water. I had a good day in the shop. I would like to have ten more years of this life, it couldn't be bettered. Ten years? There is life eternal. *1963*

The zest and urge for woodcutting is gone with the cold weather, but I enjoyed working on the sunny hillside, away from the muddy riverbank, with dry crisp leaves underfoot and the sound of the brook coming up from below. I think of summer, overcast with foliage. Now one can look up through the stretching trees to the sky, and the sun shines down through the bare branches unhindered. *1964*

March 17 An hour's satisfactory painting can be the fruition of many days, even if it vanishes after further work; but if the results are solid and lasting, the painting is the highest reward. *1961*

Yesterday evening to Hanover to hear the choir singing. It was a spring-like evening, children out playing under a full moon. *1965*

March 18 A pair of phoebes about the house, singing their reedy notes. *1954*

We are more and more pleased with Louisville. Jefferson Street (East) is amazing. Open air markets, a whole row of butcher shops. . . . At one corner we were behind a rickety wagon, driven of course by a Negro. Before they could start up to cross the intersection, the horse began to urinate, taking a long time for it, traffic waiting all the while. *1954*

The days seem unproductive and I labor to get even small things done. And there is so much to do, so much not even begun. But it is not right when I work hard and fast, and take myself too seriously. *1956*

Noticed some dandelions sprouting, and found some "wild corn" on the south slope above the creek, also one plant of wild beet; so we will have the first salad of wild greens for supper. *1963*

March 19 Bloodroot blooming now, the truest spring flower. *1956*

Anna saw a coot up the back water, having a great time all by itself. *1956*

My whole morning given to firewood, very satisfactory and enjoyable. *1965*

Yesterday to Madison, with lunch on the riverbank at Vevay, where we had gone on a sudden inspiration, to get some wheat germ (4 lbs. all they had 40 cents) from the City Roller Mills. The town is nicely kept, looks clean and neat even in winter. We were amused at one gardener's attempt, apparently, to mulch with corn shocks. The March wind had blown them all over the neighborhood. *1965*

Painting yesterday afternoon and today, achieving nothing. I rarely do, and then by chance, by a fortunate combination of circumstances. I have no style, no method, no procedure—except in my mind. When at work it always goes the same way. The habits of a lifetime are hard to break, they say. *1966*

March 20 Today we removed the paintings, drawings, and prints from the walls of Classic Hall, Hanover College, where they have hung since Feb. 20. I feel that the appreciation of them has been sincere, that they have given pleasure to many, students and teachers alike. We now have many good friends at Hanover, in fact everyone there has shown a friendly feeling towards us. Yet how glad we are to get away, to return to the unpaved and untrimmed earth. *1954*

March 21 The softness and gentleness of spring, transforming the wintry hillside, the subdued colors glowing in the rain. *1955*

I go up the hill for three goats and am rewarded by a choice song sparrow's song—very clear and melodious—three long notes, then some just a little shorter, and lower in pitch, then the quick descending ones. *1961*

Today I saw an animal swimming upstream close to the shore, making a wake and steering around drift and trees, never pausing; as if he were on a cruise. It must have been a muskrat, but looked large, with a long tail floating astern. It is cheering to think of this other life going its own way, regardless of man. *1961*

To Louisville for a concert, leaving late in the morning with a roadside lunch. . . . Returned home just at nightfall. The music was worth the trip. Also, these concerts have an added value. They take us out into the world, where we see and talk with people. This gives us an objective view of our life here, and breaks up the pattern for a brief period. *1963*

Sometimes I question the value of music, of all art. A robin sang a free and happy song while the musicians inside played their conventional sonatas. *1963*

This is the best time in a garden, when all is hope and great expectations. The earth has a newness which becomes tarnished by mid-summer, the air is fresh and warm, fragrant with the moist earth. *1966*

I hauled manure to the next garden plot for a while, then went into the studio where to my great satisfaction I achieved substantial results. Tomorrow I will probably lose it all, but the direction is clear, the goal attainable. *1966*

March 22 The day is like a game or a puzzle. You color patches of time with different moods, shape each one by some sort of action, and put them together to make the whole. The pattern of each day varies, no two are the same. *1963*

We burned winter fires this morning, the afternoon was warmed by the bright sun. *1963*

River falling a little now. I cruised about the backwater today, but soon that will be impossible. This has been a long period of inundation. It seems right that the water should be there, and land will appear strange. *1963*

A good morning in the garden, and perfect weather for it. I chop with fork and heavy hoe, overturning the green cover, exposing the rich, dark, mouldy earth, its healthy fragrance in the air I breathe, and the see-saw whistle of the chickadee, the expressive song of the cardinal. *1966*

I love my garden tools, as I do axe and saw and oars. The heavy wide-bladed hoe with short handle which I put in place of the long one it came with. The long-tined potato fork, built like a hoe, still has a long handle which I do not interfere with, or haven't yet, since it is often handy in that state. *1966*

Heard a Louisiana water thrush, first time and only once. He comes back to this hollow each spring, to sing along the running brook, open to the sky and sun; a companion in secret to me. Is he disappointed later in the summer, when the creek dries up, and he must move to the riverbank to be near water? It does not deter him from coming back the next year, for which I am thankful. *1966*

March 23 Anna baked bread, even though it was wash day. . . . What is it that sustains us in the repeated daily round? I do not mean bread, but the nourishment of the inner force that drives us. If reality is faced, there is no encouragement. *1961*

A forbidding start to the day, 40 degrees and cloudy, but it improved much, turning into a quiet sunny day which inspired me to some tentative work in the garden. It is still the great adventure and my hopes at this season as high as they ever were. I feel that I have learned something of what it takes for at least a partial realization of my hopes, but there is much I do not know or am not sure of. *1962*

I am advised to abandon these lovely hand tools whose efficiency was evolved through many generations of users, and do my garden work with a polychrome, shiny gadget which is without character, and to me very objectionable. To think of choosing to have such a contraption between me and the sweet soil, blotting out the song of birds and of the river, and the fragrances of spring. It would mean a loss of independence, because gasoline has to be brought out from town for it and if it needs repairs, a specialist must be called in. The cost is considerable, too, and the acquiring of money is slavery, for me. *1966*

March 24 I have never seen so much driftwood along our shore, blown in by the west winds, and jammed behind a heavy snag which is caught in the shallow water above the bar. Yesterday, I managed to break the johnboat out through the drift packed in behind it. Got out some of the best firewood this morning, then did a carpenter job in the goat stable. Yesterday I spread compost and hauled manure out of the stable. Most of each day is spent in this manner. Usually in the afternoon I go into the studio and paint for a little—how little it takes to balance the day. *1959*

An expedition to town today, with a long list that took us to Milton, Madison and Hanover where we collected a miscellany of items, incongruous in size and nature, but all useful to us—or the dogs or the goats. All cost money, but when you think of the complete and varied stock of the stores, painstakingly gathered together from many sources, the storekeepers might be considered as public benefactors, entitled to much greater pay than they ask. *1961*

Nothing I write gives the sense of beginning a new day, when the earth seems new created and life a dubious experiment. *1962*

Perhaps it is well we have an established routine to lean on. Otherwise, to live on this earth would be too full of terror. *1962*

A strange tendency to linger on the hilltop when the weather is dark, wet or windy. These recurring blasts of cold are good. Without them the summer would be intolerably long and hot. They hold the eager gardener in check, as they do the swelling buds, lest they get ahead of the season and the next blast freeze them. *1966*

Flowers of cottonwood are open, a noble sight in the straight-limbed rangy tree, with these dark red flowers all over it. None of summer's canopy, but the tree is open to sun and wind. Three fires burning all day. *1966*

I am no crack gardener. I am just learning the rudiments, and make serious mistakes. Yet from the beginning I have resisted the temptations of chemicals. In the time we have been gardening here, there has been a yearly improvement. There certainly was room for it, considering the ludicrous ideas I tried to put in practice in the beginning. Many disastrous failures and disappointments have been suffered. Yet each year there is plenty for us, and we have ever been optimistic and hopeful. *1966*

Why should not the gardener work with hope and faith? He puts the viable seeds in the moist fertile soil, warmed by the spring sun, not too wet, planting first the seeds of hardy plants. *1966*

March 25 Took off the first catfish, about 3/4 of a pound in weight. The fishing season is underway. *1953*

The wildflowers are the most exciting news at present. I see new ones, and miss some old friends. *1953*

The reality that our reason constructs is flimsy and in spite of our pretensions, on a small scale, it is like a candle in a room of a house while moonlight floods the earth. *1961*

March 26 We went to town. . . . Sometimes the errands in town are accomplished efficiently, with rewarding sidelights. The upstairs of the hardware store, for instance, was a fascinating place, full of disorder and possibilities. *1962*

We enjoy Roy Proffett's conversation. His roots are in a past that is gone, the old-time ways, shantyboat ways; but he lives in the present, and knows everyone for miles about. *1963*

March 27 Already my interest in gardening revives. No doubt the tiny plants and seeds feel the same way. *1953*

Wind still from the WNW but only a breath compared to yesterday's gale, the worst of the winter, I think. We burned more wood, getting up 3 times to keep the fire going through the night. . . . These are happy, busy, cheerful days for us. Extremes of weather relax the conscience. *1955*

I like to talk with Emmett O'Neal, his observations are studied and true. Talking of the Hall place, on this hillside, he said he was there once. He had lost a hound, and recognizing its voice as it hunted over here, crossed the river to see about it; explained that the dog, a friendly pup, had followed the Hall children into their boat, when he meant that the dog had been stolen. *1955*

Chill, cloudy weather. Showers yesterday, some thunder and wind. The bloodroot is compensation for the cheerless days. It could not be in summer. The bloodroot and these bare bleak hillsides, the piping of the titmouse—this is spring. I would not forego one hour of it. *1957*

When guests are here, I am, I think, gracious and friendly. I make them welcome and take an interest in them. It must be only by a great effort and displacement that I do this or seem to do it, for when the guests leave my amiability vanishes. If I know ahead of time that guests are coming, or if we are going to visit someone, making more than a brief call, I am in the same unpleasant disposition—until we arrive. *1962*

March 28 Many flowers bloom, close to the earth, mostly white. Redbud will soon break forth. Now the glow of its dark buds is almost imperceptible on the gray treed hills. The red of budding maples is astonishing; they look like a painting. The lively color of the peach blossom is seen. *1953*

Yesterday evening, while it was still daylight, we climbed the hill to R. Hamilton's carrying viola, music, stands. Our playing seemed little appreciated, perhaps the music was incomprehensible, though we thought it simple and direct. Rand played the violin part of some easy trios, and did well, though he seemed to enjoy it not at all. He did better than I could do with his kind of music. He asked, "Do you know 'The Midnight Fire Alarm'?" When Anna said, "No," he replied in astonishment, "You don't!" *1953*

No fire this evening, the sun has been warm. I worked in bare arms. How quickly and easily the mind shifts its attention from wood cutting to gardening. The fires have been my constant concern for months. Suddenly no fire is needed. Yet I take it as a matter of course. *1960*

In yesterday's mail was a request from the Guild Gallery in Louisville to remove—reclaim was the word—my paintings which have been on exhibition in the bank in the mall, so we make a trip to Louisville today. . . . To frame those pictures, transport them to Louisville, hang them on the walls, take them down and bring them home again—all this requires time and energy, not to mention skill, experience and judgment—for all this I have achieved nothing but the honor of showing my work in public, a chance to sell some of them (but none were sold) and some well-meant praise and appreciation. *1963*

The Akers family walked down the hill yesterday PM for a surprise visit. Gene has long felt a desire to "live like we do," without modern conveniences on the river, where he would build his own house, burn wood, raise a garden, fish, etc. I don't know what is behind this longing, or how deep it goes. If for moral or economic reasons, such a life would never satisfy him. Love is the only motivation that will carry through—love of the earth, rain and snow, wood fires, of your hands in the earth, of the promise of tender plants, recognition and love of goodness that surrounds us. *1963*

March 29 This quiet night, moonlight picking out the branches of sycamores, the only sound is running water in the creek. The river is quiet. *1955*

A shantyboat appeared at Lee's landing yesterday. Green cabin and red hull, it must be Bill Shadrick. We have been away from shantyboating long enough to see it as we did before living on a boat ourselves, to appreciate how unique it is, how different from ordinary ways, how compact, simple, independent. *1955*

Annie, squinting at the lamp wick she is trimming, mornings, as she washes the chimneys with the dishes. She leans over to sight the shape of the wick, scissors in hand. *1955*

This soft warm air, even the wind is warm. The struggle against the cold, the hot, steady fires I kept burning—all this is forgotten now, this temperate environment seems natural. Yet it might change in a day. *1962*

More summery weather, the morning cool, the evening hazy. Gardening this morning, planting potatoes, more spinach, more cold frames—it is moving along, there will come rain and cold, and I will cease operations, the seed will rot. *1963*

I have been thinking of the Christmas cards I used to try to make when 10 or 12 years old, a stiff white card, probably pieces of Bristol board my brother Frank had given me. I used a few stock symbols, a wreath of holly drawn in outline, the leaves colored green, with red berries and ribbon. Or a head supposed to represent Santa Claus, whose cheeks and hat I colored red. These were made with no imagination or feeling, no originality, no attempt at expression or creativeness. My painting now is much like those cards. The same subjects and treatment over and over, the steamboats in certain positions and aspects, the river, landscapes—all handled in much the same way as when I first tried them. Perhaps I should go beyond, into new fields, experiment, try new subjects, as I see now that I should have done with the trite Christmas cards. I must at least observe closer and find new symbols. The house quivers in the gale. *1964*

March 30 Bill Shadrick has beached his boat out at Lee's landing, so I guess he is there for the summer. It will make quite a difference to us, for the better, I think. . . . A dim light shines from the shantyboat window. *1955*

A chill, dreary rain this morning, and all dreams of spring have vanished. *1962*

The impressionist painters were a beginning and also an end. After them, painting lost its directness of expression, the visual and spontaneous became unimportant, the intellectual became dominant. This is the modern attitude—reactions are based on intellect and preconceived ideas instead of a response to natural, immediate experience. *1962*

Another rushing wind driving waves down the stream. They break on the bar, slap over the end of the johnboat. A sprinkle of rain now as it darkens, but streaks of light in the north promise a clearing sky. 1966

March 31 I would like to express the subtlety and grace of the landscape with primitive forms and colors.

The last day of March, a dark wet month, windy, chill, with little warm sunny weather—just March; but a time I love. 1962

April

April 1 A walk at daybreak on the hill to the north. Chill east wind, but the day became warmer with some pale sunshine. . . . I have thought of my walk all day. It is good to do something unusual or out of the ordinary, even as simple an act as this. . . . Discovered the spring which flows to the east, almost in line with the one which comes out under the bluff. Also discovered a blackberry patch and a splendid view of the river through our gap. This would hardly be expected, so far back from the river. Passing bird voices. One could spend all his time on the watch, and following after. *1956*

A stiff March wind from the west, the sky full of ragged clouds, huge masses sometimes, and shadows racing across the river. *1961*

The flowers and trees are bursting into leaf and bloom now, every day changes the landscape. *1963*

Grass is very green now, early leaves begin to green the hills and the blossoming redbud begins to show. It is an intensification of the winter color of the woods. *1964*

The weather discourages further planting, but a few of the first-planted peas are up, and the potatoes are sprouting. Warm quiet sunshine and warm showers would cause a miracle. *1966*

April 2 A long day in Louisville. . . . When the concert is half over we begin to think of the long ride home and the river crossing in the dark with some feeling of dread; but it is never so bad as it then seems; it fact, it is the most pleasant part of the day. . . . These trips which we start upon so gaily, thinking we have important business to attend to, are always disappointments and failures to some extent. We arrive home thinking we might better have stayed there. *1955*

It is 25 degrees this morning, and the wind still strong from NW. Very clear, as was last night, with an almost full moon. I would like to live forever. *1961*

There comes a time toward the end of the day when everything is done for that day, the goat chores are done, the last things are put in their places, bath and supper over, the dishes put away clean. Then we can relax thoroughly, and read, sometimes letting another think for us, entertain us. Our reading, however, is likely to be stirring, demanding; and while one reads aloud, the other is busy with some easy handwork. This period does not last long, for one or both gets sleepy, we go to bed, and arise to a busy day. *1961*

The chill days of early spring, when the grass is greening, a few birds sing with confidence, yet the blue of the sky is pale and the north wind persists. *1962*

This morning we crossed the rising river and went to Madison, where I left Anna to wait for the Cincinnati bus. She intends to return tomorrow evening. The interval of solitude is precious. It is a different world and I am a different self. I feel relieved of a responsibility that cannot be defined. I am released from pressure, my mind is free. Yet would I not feel a lack of balance if I lived alone all the time? I see Anna now as from a distance, a loving thoughtful person. She is not me, however; her desires and ideas influence our living more than mine do, in all kindness she tries to put my desires and ideas into practice, but the result is only her conception of what I am aiming at, joined with the realization of her own personality. This afternoon, I reworked the sink as a surprise to Anna and because it could be done now with no interference of her routine. *1962*

Late in the afternoon I went into the studio, with no set purpose, and after sharpening and tightening the axe on its handle, set to painting the river and hills as I saw them when crossing this morning. Working freely and happily, using a palette knife, applying the paint on the slick surface not with a plastering but with a scraping technique, I finished the picture within an hour, and now I think of it with satisfaction. *1962*

April 3 Mr. Jesse McMahan walked down to see us this morning. No doubt he likes to come, to see us and our place, to talk to us who are so interested in what he has to say, and to see this place which he knew so well when younger and which of all places has changed the least. We are honored by his coming, he is part of the earth as well as of men. *1955*

At Hanover we removed the paintings, with more nice words from the college, professors and dean. What is the result of having this group of my paintings out where they could be seen daily by many individuals? Perhaps on a very few, maybe on one or two, was an impression made. It was an advantage to me to see my pictures in a new light, through strange eyes. I still think they are good. *1961*

Another day alone. Most of the morning was given to wood gathering, cutting and wheeling. The sound of others working in their way, the diabolical whine of the power saw comes down the hill and across the river. It sounds like a mechanical monster tearing the heart out of the trees for meanness' sake. *1962*

One day last week the sycamore warbler sang, and the Louisiana water thrush, both along the creek, at the same time, as in other years. *1962*

The wild larkspur begin to bloom. *1963*

April 5 Summer heat today. I take off shirt and shoes. River almost to normal pool. I begin fishing with trot line stretched out from the bank. Wood cutting has suddenly ceased to be daily work, it is now just an occasional chore. Considerable driftwood left in the bottoms. I work at that source now. *1955*

Anna baked bread today, and I had the happy thought of making a small bread board so that the loaf could be cut at table. Thus it gets its due admiration, and the rite of cutting is enjoyed. Also there are no leftover slices. *1962*

April 6 Last night I went to Mt. Byrd church alone, in the interest of the drama "He Lives" being produced by the Sunday school class. I am supposed to help with the setting. I may have some good ideas, but no one pays any attention to them. OK with me. *1954*

These days the fireplace is still the center of life in the morning and evening, wood gathering is easy, and it is done at random. The fires are likely to be different, a little bizarre and fantastic, after the serious hard-working fires of winter. *1962*

April 7 I ponder much over Thoreau's preoccupation with friendship. He seemed to have made no practical experiments in that line. Was he, after all, lonely, and longing for companionship? His great joy is solitude, he is spiritually individual and self-sufficient. Or is he not? Perhaps his theorizing about ideal friendship is to justify his isolation, or it satisfies in a way his desire for companionship which he never enjoyed. Personally, I have no sympathy with his ideal friendship—nor do I have more friends than he had, perhaps. His self-sufficiency appeals to me more. *1961*

Sometimes I feel a need for encouragement, for certification. My own judgment of current activities and productions is not always, perhaps seldom, accurate—as I know from past experience. But on whom could I depend? *1962*

This is one of those times, perhaps just for a day and after some upheaval, or some combination of minor wrong turnings, when the progress of life seems to stop. The framework of habit and routine collapses, and nothing is accomplished. *1963*

This was the long-awaited day—sunny and warm, no wind. Gardening in earnest now, and much to do. Time to begin fishing. *1965*

April 8 After dinner I went out on the river. . . . I had hoped to make some sketches and work in the studio on my return, but nothing came of this. I have learned that this cannot be forced. The pictures strike you unawares—and you must seize them at the moment. *1962*

We had our bath a little early and played together—Beethoven Kreuzer Sonata. It was no doubt a terrible performance on my part, but we were truly inspired by the music, more than if it had been performed by *virtuosi.* *1962*

A full day, all to myself, untrammeled. I worked in the chimney garden, continuing the long effort to make something of it. I have chopped out the disappointing red raspberries, except for a half a dozen briars, chopped out the weeds to plant oats and alfalfa. If the fruit trees thrive, they will fill the enclosure and make a good showing in the eyes of the chance walker on the path. *1963*

Began another painting, not carrying it beyond the first black marks on the white panel, the most exciting stage of all. Now is hope and confidence, in the end a compromise. It is a strange life, when I consider it, how I endeavor to attain strength and clarity, to mold these base materials into forms which will express me and my attitude, my joy and thankfulness. I work alone, who cares whether I produce anything or not, or who appreciates it? Yet I believe a good thing will not perish. *1963*

Perhaps I have entered on to a new level of experience lately. My confidence, faith, have been renewed and I am inwardly happy. River has been rising, and is near top of bank. The larkspur begin to bloom, scattered and close to the ground. *1964*

April 9 Driftwood fires are different from our ordinary fires of hillside wood. The polished grooved pieces worn into odd shapes, the variety of wood, the way it burns, some pieces with flames having yellow green tips. *1955*

I do not paint with any idea of expressing my emotions. That would seem to me in bad taste. One should paint to express his joy in what he sees, and his thanks for that joy. *1962*

Now the cottonwoods are in flower, some of them showing a rich somewhat purplish red, very dark. The distant shore is colorful, but still light and delicate. Elm leaves begin to tint the hillside. *1962*

Some painting this afternoon on a larger panel. I want to make a series of large (for me) pictures. At one time, until recently in fact, I hoped to develop a manner of painting which would allow me to realize my conception dependably, a formula or system or technique in which I would know just what I was doing as step by step I constructed the picture. I know now that this is beyond hope. Each picture is an individual struggle, the outcome of which is unknown until the end. Sometimes a promising beginning is lost in further work on it. (Why did I not leave it as it was?) Sometimes by drastic measures a lost picture can be brought to life, never the same, but in a new form which is often exciting. I must paint under tension and success depends more on the spirit than on manipulation of pigment. The whole business can be so exciting, and some of the results so fine—and it can be agonized failure. *1962*

In my early days I never questioned my ideal, a life something like that we live now, only more so, seemed without doubt the only desirable and sensible way to live, the only way in which one could be happy and satisfied. I still believe all this, as sincerely as ever, but I consider it more objectively now, trying to understand the reasons why I should feel as I do, and trying to understand people to whom this sort of life is remote and undesirable. I have not arrived at any answers to my questions. Perhaps it is a waste of effort. One should live the way that is congenial to him and produce what he can. *1963*

I will remember the sky of last night. Great masses of white clouds were moving swiftly from the west, shone upon by the moon almost directly overhead. The clouds seemed charged with electricity, and lightning flashes were continuous. They lighted the undersides of the clouds which would then be for a brief instant in the shadow of the moon. Not a sound of thunder could be heard. *1965*

April 10 A warm, gentle day, windless, showery in the afternoon. No one's comprehension of life can be complete without first hand experience in gardening. The seeds we plant are like our hopes. We risk an unknown future. Gardening brings home our closeness to animals and plants, our dependence on the earth. What avails, for instance, politics? How can men be serious about the chaff they work with? *1954*

In the half light of daybreak, was it this morning or yesterday?, the song of the whip-poor-will came from up the hollow. *1963*

Learning to paint is to understand yourself so that you do not get in your own way, or spoil something good by trying to make it conform with the arbitrary pattern you have chosen. Great works of art are always spontaneous expressions. The artist does not know just how he did it. *1963*

April 11 A rainy morning, not clear yet. I walked up the north hill in the afternoon. The green slope among the trees was gay with blue larkspur, a cardinal sang, and in the open atop the hill a fragment of a rainbow gleamed in the northeast. Petty thoughts fell away and I too sang with joy. *1955*

Weather still chill and dark. It is comforting, in its way. *1958*

At the entrance to my workshop, the ground had washed out from there in the winter rains, leaving the bridge insecure. To feel it give way slightly underfoot unsettled the spirit as well, a poor approach to painting. . . . The painting left so hopefully yesterday collapsed today. *1962*

The whip-poor-will again this morning. It is a daybreak song, a wild utterance. In comparison this life is tame, the day commonplace. *1963*

April 12 Yesterday we set our bell up on a pole at the end of the terrace to the west of the house. Anna rang it today when I was across the river. It has a beautiful deep tone, and adds character and grace to our establishment. *1956*

April 13 The pattern for these days here is—work in the garden, fishing, wood gathering or other chores in the morning; some writing, often before dinner, and at suppertime; some painting in the afternoon, music together later, a bath late in the afternoon, some more fishing or stirring about doing chores at sunset. After supper we read until so tired and sleepy we must go to bed. This feeling comes all of a sudden. *1954*

Some painting this afternoon, more yesterday afternoon, exciting. Form is necessary to any work of art. The artist must master a form which suits his temperament, and what he has to say. *1962*

Yesterday to Bedford on jury duty, again tomorrow and possibly Friday. It is all bleak and unpleasant. Just to go somewhere so often is bad enough. The roads, all that one sees along the way, the new homes, the trailers, cars everywhere, advertising, even agriculture. There is little to delight one in the country. Every aspect of modern life is distasteful to me. *1965*

April 14 A frosty morning, but sunny and quiet. River rising again. Other Aprils I would be uneasy at not catching fish, which I expect to begin in March; but now with a large supply of canned goat meat we do not lack that sort of food. Also eggs are abundant and cheap (30 cents). Also I accept more readily whatever comes. *1961*

The little lizard, every summer under the planks of my wheelbarrow track along the New Road. There he was, dodging under as I passed, and summer begins. *1965*

April 15 Finished today or almost finished, an outline map of Palestine, for Elwyn E. Tilden, Jr., Professor of Religion at Lafayette College, Easton, Pa. It is to go into his new book, now being published, "Toward Understanding Jesus" (Prentice Hall). Tilden wrote about a year ago, expressing his appreciation of *Shantyboat.* No other letter from him until this recent one with the request to make the map. I suppose I was complimented by his asking, or too weak to refuse and give the time to something more worthwhile. At any rate, I said I would do the job, knowing well the troubles I would have and the time it would take. Yet now it seems right and best that I said yes. Perhaps one goes wrong only when he says no. *1956*

Last evening we went to Hanover College to see an amateur production of Sartre's "No Exit." While there, as often in such a place, in bright lights among an animated crowd dressed in indoor clothes, I looked upon myself as I would be in the morning, grubbing in the garden, wheeling manure, picking up firewood on the riverbank. The thought came that perhaps I was wasting what talents I had, and that the opinion of those people about such a life was justified. Yet when I am here out-of-doors in the free air, I am filled with love for this earth, and am satisfied with the rightness of what I am doing. Even if I did nothing else but wheel manure and grub in the garden, that would be better than any intellectual drudgery. And as for creative work, that can be done in these circumstances, by me at least, better than in a college atmosphere. *1962*

There is no need to live a life of fear and apprehension. Happiness is a natural condition, and faith is the foundation of all. *1963*

These are exciting days. Who could have imagined that this bleak winter-bound earth could bedeck herself so? *1964*

I always have several projects under way, small jobs which give me much delight. Just now I am rebuilding the loom and getting stone from the old chimney up the hollow, wheeling it in for the new construction. The trip is rather long and varied, reminding me, though in miniature, of the treks the Chinese wheelbarrow men used to take. . . . I will go on bit by bit until the chimney is all moved away. It might be thought that this slow and laborious getting together of the stone, some of it from the creek, and laying it up without mortar, because that is so difficult to procure, would hamper the stonemason and he could build a much better wall and fireplace if an abundance of stone and mortar were at hand. On the contrary, I think that these limitations, like those inherent in every art, will stimulate his imagination so that he may produce something striking and original. *1966*

April 16 We had made a trip to Madison, arriving at the Hillside Hotel about 10 AM where we displayed with difficulty five steamboat paintings for the coming luncheon. We were guests at the luncheon part of a school teachers' sorority program. I continually wonder why I let myself in for such spots, probably because of my dislike of refusing well-meaning people. (This is an excuse for my weakness, no doubt.) Also, and this is another similar excuse, I have some vague idea of saying something which will influence a receptive listener, or I hope to influence by our example. It may work out that way, in a small degree. This affair was an ordeal for both of us. *1961*

My last day in the Trimble County Court was like the first two—I was placed in the jury box, but immediately deposed because of objections from one of the lawyers. I consider myself a good juror, better than average. Perhaps that is my weakness, I am not average. My shirts and my reading in a book were against me, too. *1965*

April 17 Yesterday PM two High School boys from Madison visited us. . . . They were attracted by candle-dipping. . . . The boys took over the work and did it carefully and with evident pleasure. Anna supplemented their lunch with sassafras tea, bread, salad and other items on hand, goat milk, popcorn, and all of us ate by the fireplace. Before leaving the boys inspected the goats and helped feed the little ones. It was an adventure for them, an experience they will always remember. It would have appealed to me strongly at their age. *1961*

April 18 Our boat habits and reactions persist: when a fast moving diesel passes perhaps in the night, we set ourselves for our boat's rocking in the swells, a gentle heaving first, then violent pitching, perhaps the johnboat's bumping, or spars tripped and the hull pounding on the bank. But now our bed rests steady, and the waves pass with a swishing along the shore. *1953*

The rain turned to sleet about midday and shortly the snow began to fall—great flakes coming straight down. The river could hardly be seen through the thick air. The ground was soon white, and the snow clung to each twig and leaf. It was a strange sight, snow on the green grass and leaves, the purple larkspur rising above the snow. It was nearly a blizzard for a while, but by midafternoon the snow was over and the sun slowly shone through. Little snow was left by nightfall. Clear and still, perhaps a frost tonight. *1953*

April 19 Another bitter day, of wind and cold, snow flurries. I heard a marvelous twittering of bird song, soft, private, sung for no man's ear in the bare trees of the windy hillside. *1953*

Used Marvin Barnes' horse, Joe, the first time without one of the Barnes boys. . . . I rode Joe down. . . . We hauled 8 sled loads of sand and gravel, Anna helping with the unloading. . . .

Then in midafternoon I rode Joe back home. The riding rubbed off some of my skin. *1956*

Yesterday we were "guests" of the junior class of the Bedford High School, having been invited some time back by Mrs. Houghton, one of the teachers. The pupils seemed interested in us, asked a lot of questions, aimless and personal, were polite and respectful. Some of them exceptional young people. We had hoped to say something which would be meaningful to perhaps some of them, but I doubt now if we succeeded. At any rate I have decided—no more meetings, discussions, interviews. One is forced into a false position, and has to make statements that are not what one means exactly, or they may be untrue. *1962*

What made yesterday a day of wonders? In the warm evening, half-moon overhead, Venus bright nearby, a whip-poor-will's song from across the river in Indiana somewhere, the peeping of frogs, the fragrance of moist earth and growing things. (No sweet fragrance, like that of flowering wild grape or locust. That comes later.) The caressing mildness of the south wind, whose effect I remember from boyhood, when it caused one to leap and skip on the first barefoot days. (My friend's mother used to let him go barefoot on the day he saw the first butterfly. I have seen two recently.) All day I was teased by the song of an unseen warbler, a rising trill, perhaps the prairie, which I hear during the summer, or the parula, which I have rarely seen. I tried to see the singer, when it was near, leaning my back against a tree and looking up the hill and up into a flowering ash tree, which I discovered to be full of birds pecking around in the blossoms, strange patterns of black and yellow, then two strident bluejays flew into the tree and out, a small flock of goldfinches passed through; some smoky yellow birds, the size of cedar waxwings—what did it matter if I could not identify them? For a few moments I lived in another world, experienced life on another plane of existence, which seemed to me fair as paradise, though the birds were merely getting a living and enjoying themselves, as I was.

I spent a long afternoon in the studio, conceiving and beginning a small picture of the river as I did other work, going out now and then between showers to look across at the blue hills which glowed with the emerald of leafy buckeyes, the pale green of elms and gleaming redbud, dark cedars still showing through. The riverbank trees were a continuous line of yellow-green, each tree distinct and showing its structure. A light mist was rising from the river surface, probably caused by the heavy moist air, in contact with the cold water. The mist became a fog off Payne Hollow and a passing towboat blew a signal of three blasts. The colors of the hills were clear and strong after the rain, but their reflections were transmuted into dull gold by the muddy water, and in the sky were golden lights.

Before the showers interfered, I worked in the garden, wheeling out manure to make hills for planting melons and lima beans, breaking ground in the bottom for the first time since the high water ran off. The surface was dry and sandy, underneath the soil was damp and rich, not too wet. I planted some melons and beans, too early no doubt, they will probably rot in the cold rains still to come, or perhaps the whole bottom will be flooded again. I covered the manure with earth so that it would not wash away. The redbuds are at their best now, the wild larkspur almost so. What a spectacle! If my visitor from afar was not impressed, overwhelmed by the beauty of the earth—how green after the rains— *1964*

April 20 Old Joe, the horse, left a good impression. He was willing and considerate, sensitive to the work in hand and to my desires. He seemed to want to please, in the off hand, indifferent way of a horse. When I saw him the day before, charging free through the pasture, and sensed his power and weight, I had some misgivings. What could curb and direct him? Surely not me, whom he did not know; and sagacious as he was, he would spot my weakness at once. Yet when he ended his wild bolt, at the single pole which could be easily broken down, he allowed the smallest Barnes boy to climb on his back and Norman to lead him by a flimsy rope around his neck. *1956*

We transplanted ferns from the woods to our door yard, to mark the day [their wedding anniversary]. . . . I think of that April 20, 1943, now eighteen years past. The details are clear, the weather. Where would each of us be now, if we had not joined our lives, what would our condition be separately? *1961*

A clear frosty morning. The rare sight of the sunlight reddening the crest of the ridge, then descending like a curtain of light. *1962*

Early this morning the voice of the whip-poor-will came from far off and I thought, how many more distant songs are in the air that I cannot hear? Then a wood thrush warbled a few notes and the day was begun. *1963*

April 21 I would like to write, not in conversational form, but constructing words into forms which would have more meaning. Possibly the end would be poetry. *1961*

We play some, violin and cello. First, some Bach clavier music, then some older things, fragments of Obrecht and Tavener. It was like getting into a new country. *1962*

We went to Louisville. . . . Cities are amazing places. Who would choose to live in them, to go to them day after day. They have no beauty, they are without hope. *1964*

These are the days when the birds arrive pell mell, when the trees burst forth and the hills become green. Then it is summer. As we ate supper on the terrace (yesterday for the first time) a thrush was singing far off toward the south, perhaps on the other side of the river. *1965*

April 22 The succession of days, it seems endless. Each day we are busy, and active, there is little change or variety. Yet our life is rich and exciting. We apparently do not become weary of one another. It is amazing, how different we are, what a different world each lives in, even though our lives are dovetailed so closely. I suppose each would be shocked to know the inward and unrevealed thoughts of the other. *1962*

River falling. Where will it stop? *1965*

The whip-poor-wills sing up the hollow every evening—just now across the creek and very loud. The most remarkable bird song, perhaps. I heard them one morning at daybreak. *1966*

April 23 Saw three white birds riding a drift log. Travellers of the first order. *1953*

When I walk with other people, I see everything through their eyes, and the earth is dull. *1961*

I said that R whom I met yesterday was an antithesis of me. The men we met today in town and at the college were of the same standing. Perhaps the whole world of men is. . . . Yet I admire all these men. They are making a brave show, leaning together and helping one another by their presence, if not with intention. *1963*

April 24 Gentle rain in the night and showers all day, off and on. The big cottonwood contained a block of myrtle warblers. The stars, trees partly bare, new leaves opening, and pendant flowers, and the bright colored, flitting birds. *1953*

It is suddenly full summer. We look out from under leafy trees. *1954*

We have been reading the Thoreau journal (1840) again, mornings after breakfast in bits almost as written. *1961*

Sometime I wonder, how can I take myself seriously as a painter, I give so little of my time to it. The pictures are small and quickly done, always the same. The Chinese painters are encouraging, they dashed off their stylized work. *1962*

An invasion of visitors—all the girls of the junior class of Bedford High School, about 24, plus 8 renegade boys, plus one teacher. . . . I could think of no better way to entertain them, an obligation which Anna and I both feel strongly in such cases, than by taking them out on the river in the john-boat. *1962*

Bird song in the morning has reached quite a chorus. The hills are greening, it is quickly done, and spring is gone. The line of river trees is uniformly green, instead of red, yellow, gray, green in shades. *1962*

It is pathetic to see people, especially when young, engaged in activities supposed to be pleasurable, yet not really enjoying themselves, only forcing themselves to, going through the motions. *1962*

When I was over in the chimney garden in the afternoon, the blue-winged warbler was singing up the short-cut path, as he does every summer. Is it always the same bird? His song suggests the heat of summer. The Kentucky warbler was singing too, reminding one of leafy coverts sheltered from the sun. *1964*

April 25 The hillsides are in summer green now. The flush of color in the opening, when the trees are all each one different, when the hills show much purple, red and orange, is as brief as the color of sunrise. *1955*

I spent a good part of this rainy day grinding cornmeal, wheat flour, soybeans and sunflower seeds. Once I considered the grinding rather as a gesture, but it takes on a new significance, becomes more essential, really the only source of honest food. We could go further. *1955*

To get up on a morning in this season, even a cloudy one like this is, is to be created new. The earth is vibrant with life. All our senses are caressed. *1961*

April 26 The greening of the hillsides is spectacular, they are in their most exciting state, each tree showing individual texture and color, many red and yellow hues. *1961*

River rising. The rain scoured out the creek and carried away both my bridges. *1961*

Visitors at evening, a young couple. . . . Many such (young, a tendency toward culture, no aim or conviction but with a sympathy toward experiments in natural living, dissatisfaction with present conditions and ways of living, a feeling that many people are not living successful lives, inwardly, and that their own lives will be unsuccessful, whatever step they take). They are not inclined to live as we do, nor have they the required manual skill, or interest in that direction. Hard work of any kind does not appeal. *1964*

April 27 A fair warm day. I work in the garden, most of it; some in shop. White and colored lilac in bloom, the latter scents the air. The hawthorn is white. *1961*

One of the paintings brought here from Fort Thomas was done on canvas, in the 1920's, I would say, a sort of vignette since an irregular border of bare canvas surrounds the picture. I made it one wintery morning, rather I saw and conceived it then, looking down on the river from the railroad at Brent. Above a surface of fog on the river, the sunrise color shows in the sky and a suggestion of a far hill. The sunrise color is reflected in the water along shore, which is irregular and lined with bare willows. A strip of level bottom land inside the willows is covered with snow. Here two small shantyboats are beached out, close to the bottom left hand corner of the picture, a warm light showing in the window of one boat, smoke coming from its stovepipe, and the snow is already partly melted from its roof. I feel that I could not now make that picture, so direct and innocent. I consider it good. What I make now might look good to me 35 years from now, but in a different way. *1962*

April 28 How summery now. In the evening, I row across in the calm, in the fading light. *1953*

A rough day, unpleasant to be out, but exciting. *1961*

East wind, mild, hazy sun. The nights are silent as winter, unless a whip-poor-will calls. I listen, and in the silence create the sound of insects which should be heard under the leafy trees. *1963*

April 29 The first chat today. . . . The larkspur, phlox, bluets are fading but the vast fields of them along the creek are a magnificent sight. *1953*

Cloudy this morning, as it was yesterday, but the promised showers are withheld. As I worked in the sand bottom yesterday planting soybeans, I listened to a continuous polyphony of bird song from all sides, warbling, twittering, regular and improvised whistles, chirps and repeated noises, amazing after the silent woods and fields of winter. *1962*

April 30 It is as difficult for me to change my habits of painting as it would be to change my mind or body; yet I see glimmerings of a new light at times. Will it ever be understood or realized? *1956*

To attain your principles, to live by them, to defy the world, that would be a stirring life. But what of these people to whom you are attached, and obligated? They do not share your principles, perhaps they have none. Who has, except for narrow rules of conduct which fit in with the turn of their minds, with their likes and aversions? Should these people be defied, too? Or can we be satisfied with merely believing in our principles, while acting against them for the sake of others? This has been my problem all my life. *1961*

May

May 1 Several times I have carried with me through the day a scrap of paper and a pencil with which to note stray thoughts which I might not remember until evening; but the plan was never successful and was soon abandoned. However, I started again today. It occurred to me that perhaps this writing is all that I will ever do, and I should make the most of it, being careful to record every word or idea. *1962*

If I should live to be a hundred, I would still feel that the best lay ahead, that my best work would still be done—and this would not be a dream or desire, but would be certified by living faith. *1962*

The gentle rain comes straight down
On the mud and withered grass and sodden leaves
There is no sky, no wind,
There is no distance
The mind turns inward
Oh why should I be so happy
About the stark trees and the mist?
My destiny will be a joy. *1962*

May 2 Almost summer now. I smelled the cedars in the warm sun, the dry, scented air of high regions. *1953*

I look down now on the level bottom which I intend to plant in garden, to make vegetables grow there in place of the weeds that are flourishing now. How green they are! They would grow up into a magnificent weed forest. Who has figured out the succession of weeds, why one kind predominates, another kind the next year? It seems a task for Hercules to effect this thwarting of nature, with no help from men or machines. *1961*

Roy Proffett visited us today, after a long absence. He arrived just as we were starting to eat dinner, and without hesitation or excuse, sat down at the table to share what we had. That I regard as a compliment, an act of friendship. *1962*

May 3 Full summer, one might say. The green trees overshadow the earth. *1965*

Painting must wait until the garden does not demand work on it, whenever that time shall come. Yet the days have many leisure moments and are unhurried. A short nap during the day allows us to read some by lamplight. And we play music daily, unless visitors interfere, as they did the past Sat. and Sunday. *1965*

May 4 I am certain that the goats awake and look forward with joy to roaming the green woods and hollows by circling paths, nibbling favorite leaves, resting in the shade when the sun becomes warm. *1960*

We adapt ourselves to the almost continuous noise of engines and are only at times conscious of it. Even here, which is considered a quiet place, the river boats, tractors, airplanes, pleasure boats, even distant power lawn mowers, power saws, cars and trucks. Last Sunday for the first time I heard a church bell, probably from Paynesville. That was a good sound, so was the song of the olive-backed thrush. Each year at this time he spends a few days on our hillside north of the goat shed, where he seems to sing for my private delectation and encouragement. *1961*

May 5 Sometimes the birds look in through our windows. They seem not to see us. The Carolina wren often come close. Today it was a Bewick wren, singing a few feet away. *1953*

Rain began shortly after daybreak and it was a thoroughly wet day; but now the clouds are breaking and some sunset color shows in the west. Some days are heroic, when you see everything clearly—your course ahead, your relations with other people, life itself. I feel that I am a stronger person than I was this morning, and that my life has reached a higher plane. *1961*

This I have decided—not to sell another painting. If someone really wants one, I will give it to them. *1961*

Last night was the first summer night, complete with chirping of crickets, the dreaming of frogs, the mingled odors of blossoms (locust) and fresh leaves, the mild, balmy air, a moon three quarters full making a gleaming white sky of the thin clouds. *1963*

May 6 I mowed the last of the rye planted last fall as a cover crop. It has been a constant joy as a band of dark, rich green on the winter hillside, a waving field of tall grass, becoming paler as it approached the harvest. . . . In cutting it I am reminded of mowers cradling the harvest. The whole process done by hand would be beautiful. How much has been lost to the tractor and combine. Yet did the men using cradle and flail appreciate or enjoy the beauty of their work? They are the same ones using the machinery today, glad to escape the long, hard drudgery. *1954*

Painting is arduous and difficult as mountain climbing. People think it a pleasurable pastime. *1961*

The world, represented by _____ _____ and three of his young helpers, with a tractor, scraper and power saw, actually made a path to our door through the wilderness, removing fallen trees, filling in the deepest holes, and cutting down the steepest banks. I am afraid that their motive was not a seeking for excellence but mere curiosity. *1962*

This must be the season of most abundant bird song, with all the local residents singing lustily, and migrants passing through. The white-throated sparrow heard recently, the gray-cheeked thrush still with us, rose-breasted grosbeak and others. Some of them I notice only for a day, as the redstart yesterday. Finest of all has been the occasional night song of a sweet-voiced bird, perhaps the vesper sparrow. It sings rarely night or day, and I have not been able to see it, though I heard it near the house in daylight. *1962*

The river calm, as brilliant as the sky, the frogs and crickets chanting for joy. *1963*

May 7 The work _____ _____ and crew did on the road made it quite passable for a tractor, even a truck, and it is in better shape than for several years. Yet I can't say that I appreciate the work, or like the road better. *1962*

May 8 I wonder if any of the busy farmers have as much work on hand as I have. I want to give all my time to whatever I begin the day with. Yet it must be left, and another taken up, then another. All the threads must be kept going. That which suffers is my painting, which is sulky, demanding all or nothing. *1955*

On Sundays we let our work lay, not from religious scruples, but just to show we can; and to conform with local custom. *1955*

The season of the whip-poor-will. We have never heard so many in this neighborhood. . . . Such a solid, confident, powerful sound to come from the night, and yet it expresses the mystery and unearthliness of darkness. *1955*

The day has been dark and cold, with light showers. Extreme weather upsets the even course of our living, like sickness. The compensation for the cool wind is the pleasure of real fires, which burn all day. *1960*

This is a day to write about. Heavy rains during the last night and most of today. When I looked out at the river at daybreak, I saw it half up the bottom along the shore, only the nose of the johnboat showing, far out in the yellow water. It was not raining at the time. Taking off pants and underwear, I waded out and would have had to swim, except that some overhanging sycamore branches let me pull myself over to the boat. I could not untie the stern line, had to go back to dry land for my knife, which I carried out to the boat in my teeth. Oars and floorboards are gone, but I found everything, and some planks used to walk on, a short distance downstream in some drift caught by trees and the fence. We lost nothing. . . . This evening the river stands at 22½ feet, rising. *1961*

May 9 All the bottom land is covered, the old road is going under. It is sad to see my planting submerged, peas with sticks, even the tiny alfalfa and rape plants. The numerous loads of mulch that I hauled from the fence, where it was caught in the last rise out onto the garden, has been swept away, over the fence this time into the woods. Such is gardening on the riverbank. I transplanted the strawberry plants from the old road, and the small tomato plants from the cold frame into boxes, the cold frame itself has gone on a voyage. *1961*

A Hanover student here all day. He walked both ways to Lee's landing, helped me in the garden this morning. It is a burden to me and his assistance is not worth the time of mine that he wastes. The giving is on my side, after all. *1964*

No painting the past week, or little satisfactory activity of any kind. I expect the same next week, but it will swing the other way in time. *1964*

May 10 We went on to Hanover, where Anna took the bus to Cincinnati. . . . This evening I feel a new quality to aloneness, like the stars shining after all the dark and stormy weather. *1961*

I felt really ill, but was not alarmed, and today I am in great elation of body and spirit. *1963*

Now the fragrance of wild grape blossoms is heavy in the air as one approaches certain shores. The day-long singing of the wood thrush is our delight. No other music could approach its calm serenity. *1963*

We viewed hastily the showing of contemporary graphic art. I was little attracted but I feel more and more my isolation. *1963*

May 11 Emmet O'Neal caught quantities of large carp in the backwaters, he brought in 35 or 40 to us, which we canned, smoked, took up the hill and put in a live box. The smoking was a failure, due to bad judgment on my part, also to heat, rain, company and rising river, which flooded the smoker. *1958*

Emmet O'Neal pulled in with a boat load of carp for us, according to his promise of yesterday. He would not accept any money for them. This is another example of the abundance that comes our way—and of the hours of labor we put in. I worked until milking time on those fish. *1961*

I fall down now and then but seldom am hurt because of

my light weight and agility. This morning, running on the dry steep hillside to head off a goat, I lost my balance, fell, rolled over and was on my feet in seconds. However, I struck my ribs against a small stone which just about put me *hors de combat.* *1963*

May 12 A steamboat whistle sounded downriver, a boat making its way through the fog. It did not blow 3 mechanical toots, like the diesels, but it was like 3 organ notes, muted by the fog. I guessed what boat it was; we had seen advertisements for the excursion boat *Avalon,* for Madison on May 12, today. Soon it steamed slowly by, but a few rods off shore, smoke rolling from its stacks. *1953*

Another dark, chill day, sky breaking in west at sunset. . . . We should be thankful to be alive, reasonably active and out of pain. *1960*

Last night to Hanover College to see their production of "The Rivals." I enjoy the theatre, and can enter into a play completely; yet I feel no desire to see more plays, or to see any. *1962*

What a grinning simpleton I am! Yet if I showed my true face, few if any friends or visitors would come to us. *1962*

A wonderful year for locust bloom. One could hardly believe that those gaunt spare trees could attain a flowering. Those two in our garden have been filled with humming insects and their fragrance drifts about. *1964*

Now the riverbanks are sweet with blossoming wild grapes, heavy and cloying. How come I have never read of it, in poetry or the writings of naturalists? It should figure in mythology. *1964*

Last night, when no one saw or heard, the big cottonwood at the mouth of Buck Run toppled into the river. . . . Many trees have been washed out in the past few years. I believe it is due to the increase in size, speed and number of the diesel towboats, which roll in breaking waves, often several times a day. *1965*

May 13 No painting for several days, except for a few intense moments. *1961*

When I went out under the trees last night, heard the chirping of the first crickets, the dreaming trill of frogs, just as the yellow moon rested on the far hills, there seemed such peace, serenity and comfort in the unfolding night, with its soft scented air. *1962*

May 14 We went to Madison this morning to hang the paintings in Hammack's store, 22 of them, about 6 done recently, some older ones, some very old from my stock in the Fort Thomas studio. All but 4 or 5 were never shown before. Putting all these pictures in such a public place, or any public place, is like baiting a fish line. One never knows what he will catch, probably nothing. Many a fish will sniff or nibble at the bait and not be at all tempted to swallow it, he will even possibly offer adverse criticism. What a joy it would be if someone saw them who could see in them the good that I see. No one has ever appreciated them for what I believe them to be. Probably no one ever will. Perhaps I am mistaken in their value. But I know of none other that would better express what they are intended to express. *1962*

All the hours we worked in the store this morning the radio brayed the music and voices of an idiot world. No one paid any heed to it, which is well, for otherwise they would go mad, too. *1962*

May 15 This is real summer. Tonight the house seems warm and it is most pleasant to go out into the cool fresh air. *1962*

One of the joys of summer, comparable to that of open fires in winter, is the copious drinking of fresh cool water, and going into the water bodily, not only cooled but supported and gently massaged by it. Today twice, noon and evening. *1962*

These are low days, with low thoughts and crude work. *1963*

May 16 From what I observe of Hanover students, I would say that young men do not rely on themselves. Their ideas come from current movements, the carrying out of their plans depends on established organizations. There seems to be a growing desire to do "service" work. Perhaps it was always so, or it may reflect the decline of the individual. *1961*

May 17 Yesterday the stern-wheel gas towboat *Sandy* passed down. . . . Some 12 or 13 years ago it picked up Frank [Harlan's brother] and me when we were paddling down the Kentucky in a canoe and took us to Carrollton. *1953*

The peewee sings his simple plaintive notes through the day, but in the evening, after the sun has set and the light is fading, this bird sings after all the others are silent, expanding his whistle into ecstatic melody. Perhaps he feels alone in the world then, and such is the effect of solitude. *1962*

In ordinary conversation, I am dull and stupid, giving out nothing, taking in all that is said, to go over it in my mind later, recalling every word and inflection, also the expression on the speaker's face, the hidden overtones of meaning. It is then I think of what I might have said, which no doubt would have been interesting to the hearers. Only at rare times can I speak out, and then the subject must be near to me. At other times and most frequently, I must constrain myself to the viewpoint of others, feeling that they have no interest, no conception of my true self. *1963*

It is remarkable how worldly people are, concerned only with society. Is not one man by himself important and worth consideration? To me he is worth sacrificing the whole world for. *1963*

On Saturday I committed one of those blunders. Having crossed the river to meet arriving guests, I landed at the foot of the boat-launching ramp, the two passengers being at the top. Hastening to assist them. . . . I stepped out of the boat without fastening it. I think it was the dogs jumping out that pushed the boat away from shore. When I looked it was out of reach, moving farther in an offshore breeze and drifting downstream. I hastened out on the roots of the big trees there, but saw that reaching the boat was hopeless. I tossed off boots and socks and shirts, plunged in and swam 30 or 40 feet to reach the boat. Water was not too cold, but I was, on the return trip. *1966*

May 18 Heavy rains in the night, and now in the reluctant dawn it pours down through the heavy foliage. This is discouraging weather for the farmer, and for the gardener, too. I can set it all aside and rejoice in accomplishments that would be impossible if I were gardening heavily. *1961*

Sometimes I feel a longing to travel, to pass through new country, a free and independent, self-contained unit, with nothing more to do than to see, reflect and compare, make notes and sketches, a stranger, whom the natives ignore. Travel in these days means autos and highways, and that no longer appeals to me. Perhaps travel in a foreign land? But then I would be a tourist. *1962*

The earth is showered now with cotton from the cottonwood trees. The smooth surface of the river was flecked with it and the level plane of the water was made evident, and our passage over it. *1962*

May 19 Our return to the Ohio River from Michigan was memorable. After driving southward over level sunny country, we entered a region of storm clouds and wound down into the river valley. Here it was hot and sultry. We sensed the river and its land. The storm broke. Reaching Lee's landing, we found the lane and path almost dry; it was out of the storm's path. A hurried crossing in an ominous calm, a storm crossing the river at Saluda Creek at the same time. *1954*

The river is getting a summery look, the less muddy water reflecting the green trees and hills, the trees so heavy with foliage you expect them to break. *1961*

May 20 A writer on Art may say, Paint the nature of a thing, not the appearance. In my painting the appearance is everything. It is the appearance of the subject which attracts me, its form, color, texture. I love what I see to such an extent that I would not change a particle of it. Yet because of limitations of material and skill one must arrange, choose and simplify. *1961*

May 21 My life in all its aspects is closely involved with the weather. *1962*

Yesterday to Hanover and Madison. We delivered the painting commissioned by the college, a rendering of the river scene from the campus ($175, the highest price I have so far received for a painting). *1966*

May 22 The locusts are beginning to sing, like the first musicians of the orchestra to take their places, tuning up. *1953*

I meet several toads in the course of the day, when mowing, raking or hoeing, and they are good friends, the most harmless creatures, trusting, or maybe they have to be, since it is not in their power to get away quickly. Yet they never seem to get hurt, even when in the grass I am mowing. Their size and color varies, but they may be all of a kind as far as I would know. One of their retreats is under the boards on which we walk to and from the river. As you step along, several toads will hop out from hollow places in the earth, where it is shady, damp and cool. *1962*

No visitors today—a respite. Yesterday and the day before we had no time for ourselves in the afternoon. On Wed. morning I went across after the bell rang and was greeted by 5 members of the senior class of Madison High School who had come to buy one of my paintings, a gift to the school from the senior class of 1964. I enjoyed these unpretending, direct young people. They selected a suitable picture, a good choice, for which I asked $75, less than they had expected to pay. *1964*

May 23 Some of our visitors make remarks which should be remembered—Mrs. Cary Robertson, in her dry plain way, "You have all the conveniences of the nineteenth century." Mel Bookout, Hanover student: "A visit to your place should be part of every Hanover student's education." *1960*

The tractors are running early and late—corn planting, I suppose. . . . What effect does a tractor have on the nature of the man driving it? The sound of a tractor is unpleasant and disturbing. A team of horses would bring a man closer to the earth, it would not interfere with anyone's communion with nature. *1960*

For myself, I want to drop the seeds in a furrow I have made with a hoe, smelling the earth, listening to the song of birds. That is why I make a garden. *1961*

I began painting this afternoon, after a long interval, just as if there had been no interruption. Yet I always find some new element, though perhaps I am not aware of it, or know what it is, until I begin to paint. Prolonged and continuous production is impossible with me. Even if I force myself to work at it, the results show signs of the seed running out. *1962*

May 24 The fragrance of wild grape is in the night air. The nights are wonderful. The cool fresh air, full of odors and insect sounds, with a large moon now—yet we sit indoors, reading by a smelly lamp. When I get up in the middle of the night sometimes, and am greeted by the dogs who have been sleeping on the grass, I think they are wiser than we are. . . . In the evening the frogs are heard from every direction, and overhead in the trees, yet toward morning, except for some crickets, the night is silent. *1962*

I must be more versatile in fishing. The fish are there all the time, but they cannot be caught in the same way all the time. Fishing is not part of my nature, yet I enjoy what we do of it. *1962*

May 25 A summer day. To Madison in the morning. . . . The town is unbelievable. It could not be invented by the most imaginative mind, yet it is lived in without question. Its strangeness and unreality become more apparent to me, after living in the "country." *1961*

The most exciting bird song is the peewee's, when he sings in ecstasy as night falls, repeating his song over and over. *1961*

Surely that person is fortunate who has something—anything—that he really wants to do, about which he can think constructively—and dream about it, too. An artist, a true one, is above everyone else. *1963*

May 27 Painting on a small picture. The real painting is done in a very short time. It is a sort of bursting into flower. *1963*

May 28 A storm came up. . . . I spent the afternoon in the shop, too dark during the storm to paint, so I worked on the wheelbarrow. I thought it was finished but Anna's sharp eyes detected a fault which must be corrected. This will not be difficult. *1963*

May 29 I sometimes doubt our ability to live here, this way, especially for Anna. For her it is a life of drudgery and deprivation. Nor does she have the joy and satisfaction that I do, or thought I did. *1953*

I went up the hill this morning, picked a bucketful of strawberries from M. Barnes' patch. . . . It was pleasant to step along a road, to see it winding and swinging from side to side ahead of me, up and down. *1962*

The young wildlife suffers many tragedies. I heard a squeaking inside the goat yard, saw in the grass a large blacksnake crushing a nest of baby rabbits. *1962*

How good it is to write or paint without a thought of criticism from anyone, or of pleasing anyone. The critics overreach themselves, they do not know as much as they think they do. *1965*

May 30 After [guests] 3 days and nights we are alone again. I rise to the surface, dazed, but happy to get on my true course again. To know something of another's life, of a family's life, is an amazing revelation. How much a human being can stand, and accomplish, day after day, never quite happy or well, never unified, always pursuing some distant goal with considerable zest and hope. *1961*

These are empty days, much time being taken up by visitors and garden work. No painting since May 19, but then— *1966*

May 31 I worked hard in the garden most of the afternoon, had just ceased and was on my way to the studio when a boat arrived belonging to a Hanover student, with 3 more students and 2 professors. When they left it was time for milking. *1961*

In the leafy woods there is so much contrast to the sunlight that the shade is like twilight, like going down into a deep ravine. The pale green of the jewel weed is ghostly, tall stems and leaves lying horizontally to catch all the light possible. Then to hear the thrush singing on the hill above. *1962*

A busy afternoon. Some painting—how easy it is sometimes. *1962*

Cool nights and mornings, fog this morning. Tonight the frogs are noisy, apparently in the creek, the crickets chirp loudly. In these days the fragrance of wild grape and honeysuckle flowers drift through the air. . . . I often hear a bluebird down toward the landing. *1965*

Summer

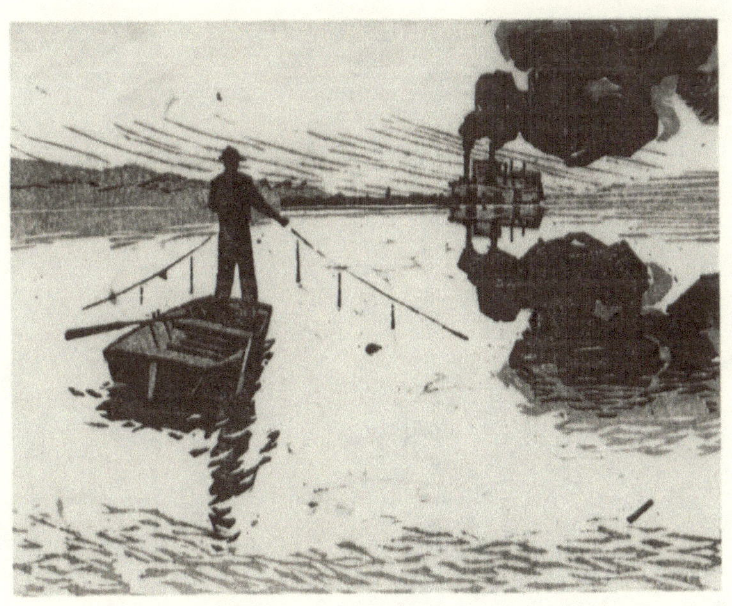

June

June 1 Last night was the first warm night, and today was quite hot, with a strong, dry wind from SW. The sound of frogs on a summer night. *1961*

"To be voluntarily poor is to have rejected what we cannot both admire and use." [From Coomaraswamy; see June 2 entry.] There is much connected with my life which I do not admire or consider beautiful. I long to get rid of it. *1961*

There is a fragrance drifting about. You enter and leave currents of it as you go along the paths. It must be from blooming wild grapes. *1963*

Company solid all day yesterday and this afternoon. Think how much I could have done in that time. But perhaps being cordial to visitors is as important as gardening. *1963*

June 2 In the quotation from Coomaraswamy [June 1 entry], I would substitute "love" for admire. *1961*

I treasure any piece of iron or other metal I pick up, as a savage would. . . . I find bits of iron from former inhabitants—a horse or mule shoe, a clevis, an iron dog used to fasten log rafts together, rusty chain, square spikes, drift bolts, rings from harness, etc. The chassis of a buggy lay near the river, perhaps pushed over the bank there. *1961*

The human body is the most beautiful and efficient machine ever devised. It is a joy to use it. Mind, spirit and the body itself benefit from use. With the aid of a few simple tools, themselves as old and natural as the body, much can be accomplished. Yet the whole desire and tendency of the human race is to substitute other machines for the body, a great loss in efficiency, nor is there any joy in this or satisfaction. *1961*

I have often seriously considered buying some power equipment to help me with the heavy work here—in the summer it would be a gasoline-powered "tiller" for gardening. Often I have been on the point of deciding to get one, I have been just recently, but always have shied away and held to the old way, more from aesthetic, ethical and sentimental than for practical reasons. As for myself, I will use the timber till it breaks, as Thoreau says. As for the garden, I will do what I can; the rest will be undone. This decision is practical, too. For machines cost more than they are worth; if not in money, they do in trouble and disturbance. *1961*

Friday evening we went to Madison. . . . The town seemed as innocent, happy, relaxed and friendly as the summer twilight. People walked along the sidewalks, went in and out of the stores, all of which were open. The colored cars glided along the smooth streets and friendly greetings were heard. . . . Yet the song of the thrush was not heard, nor could one see an expanse of sky. The twilight deepened into night, and we rowed across the river in darkness, seeing only the sky, the masses of the hills. I thought of nights in camp. *1962*

June 3 "Wilmer's" light [navigation light on shore, for guiding towboats] has been changed from oil to a flashing electric. When we first came here the Harts Falls light and the Spring Creek light were oil burning, and we were surprised to find them, having seen none on more familiar shores for quite a few years. Perhaps there are none left on the Ohio now. It is a distinct loss for us, not to see the mellow glow up the river. *1957*

Light rain this evening, after a hazy, sultry day. Some chopping in the garden this morning, a sweaty job; then visitors. The rain is good, it washes all that away. The future is without a cloud, not even a haze. . . . Made a crossing today with 8 passengers and myself, a baby and a dog. *1963*

On our trips to town, we observe many people, some of them quite closely, for a brief time. Because we see so few people as the days pass here, they make a deep impression. . . . Ordinarily people see too much of people. Yet they all like it that way, and bring shades of almost imagined people into their lives, and bodiless voices. *1964*

June 4 The false grimaces a man puts on his face, the thoughts of which he represses utterance. The universal amiability and good nature of people. How can there be discord in this world? An expression of dissent is to be cherished. *1952*

Caught 8 catfish last night, only one of them small, and a large gar. . . . One of the catfish got away as I was transferring them to the box. I was a little vexed at myself as it slithered away, yet glad to see it free. *1962*

This place seems something of a wilderness apart from the busy world, but if you could look down on it from some high point, the wilderness part would look very small compared with the cultivated area that hems it in. On all sides are fields, roads and houses. The river is a thoroughfare of commercial traffic, a speedway for pleasure boats. Madison is not far away, Hanover College, Louisville. A main highway is less than 5 miles west, and the roar of its trucks reaches our ears, we hear the diesel engines of the towboats, tractors in every direction, power lawn mowers, power saws, machines working in the gravel pit across the river. We ourselves are part of this world, more than we or our friends realize. *1964*

June 5 White down from cottonwood trees drifts through the air like large snowflakes, and sometimes the bare ground is whitened. The opened pods hang from the trees like white flowers, an impressive sight on the old, dying tree by the creek. *1956*

The days always begin with a heavy morning fog but are fair nevertheless. The steady rain of last Friday night was beneficial. We are grateful for it as for the favor of a god, though it is the blind and impartial working of the natural system. *1961*

Often it seems that no one but myself has anything pressing to do, or any work that they want passionately to accomplish; nor is the time precious to anyone but myself, and so much of it wasted or demanded by others. All this is not true, I know, but labor by hand alone impresses one with the value of time. *1961*

I think I saw the first green heron. *Yes.* Where do they spend April and May? We do not see them then. *1961*

Thinking of the two children here last week, 6 and 9 years old, I wonder if they will see such great changes in human living as I have seen since I was their age. If so what direction will those changes take, and what unforeseen developments will there be? I am sure that never in their life will those children forget the river as it is now, the barges, the catfish and john-boat. *1961*

What good is an artist anyway? His work may give pleasure to a few who are in the know, but not to all such. They pick and choose, praise or condemn, according to their tastes. Cannot a work of art have universal meaning, and be admired by all people? *1961*

Now in the twilight the thrush is singing. I do not hear it now, but the ecstatic singing of the peewee as darkness falls must be mentioned again. He seems to be trying to express all the happiness and satisfaction of the day into those last minutes of daylight. Yes, I hear it now, beyond the measured cadences of the thrush. *1963*

June 6 Last night at bedtime the sky was clear, a young moon low over the western hills. I watched the fireflies as I looked down into the bottom land, like a basin in its wall of dark trees, all filled with the flashing, moving light. Nowhere, I believe, are there so many, so brilliant. Their wild dance suggests the supernatural. The scientist would explain it probably as the mating of insects, but how would he account for the joy it raises in the beholder? That is the supernatural part, and it can't be explained away. It is more real than the scientific fact. I was awakened by heavy rain in the night, and as often at that time I felt a fear and dread of the power of the elements. The rain slackened, I went out. . . . There was no wind, in the dark sky lightning flashed incessantly, thunder sounded. The fireflies were more brilliant than earlier, in their dark amphitheater, and they seemed the sparks of some wild frenzy. *1962*

This good rain, which began as a storm in the afternoon, still falls, steady and straight down. All growing things rejoice, and the farmer. *1965*

Today was one of those Sundays—4 visitors by boat this morning, 15 on horseback this afternoon. *1965*

June 7 June: I sweat away while I mow the lush, rank-smelling weeds, pestered by mosquitoes, the whistling of birds from all sides, the air hazy; loose, low clouds in the pale sky, all colors are dull and flat. This is our nearest to the tropics. All vegetation flourishes, the animals droop. I am full of joy to be part of it. *1961*

I think that our way of living, if not a reversion, or attempted going back to old and abandoned ways, is contrary to the course of the cultural evolution they talk about. From that fact comes the difficulty. It is sad to think that man can no longer live a simple, natural life, but must depend on the chemist, engineer and technologist for his elemental needs. That which began as a luxury has become a necessity, and he cannot face his environment without these artificial aids and protections. *1961*

There seems to be a spirit of good will and friendliness among all people, when they meet and talk together. *1961*

I drink a large quantity of water during these summer days. . . . I usually go into the river twice a day and often have a warm bath inside with Anna. When the creek is running, I stop many times when crossing to bathe my hands, arms and face. Best of all is the constant view of the river, refreshing to the spirit. *1962*

The garden is at its lowest point now. The enthusiasm and hope of planning and planting is over, the plants are struggling against weeds, bugs, disease and adverse weather, though of course they are aided by sun and rain and their inherent virtue. *1962*

I haven't much in common with the steamboat experts, collectors of old photographs, etc. They think my paintings are too sketchy, preferring hard detail, whether a work of art or not. If they like the *Delta Queen,* or even the *Tom Greene,* I can't respect their taste. I try to express the life and character of the steamboat, not its skeleton. It is a symbol, of just what I do not know, rather than an end in itself. *1965*

The frog is an earthy voice which could have sounded in the primitive wilderness before man's disturbance. The song of the thrush and peewee seem to come from more open woods and clearings. I try to imagine what this fair landscape which I view was like before openings were made in the forest, before there were fields and the variety of color and texture which cropland gives to a rural countryside. *1965*

I yearn for the wilderness and lean towards it, yet perhaps it is a retreat into which one retires only for a time, to gain strength and assurance when the world presses him too hard. *1965*

As I write, I look out through the open doors down over the flourishing garden to the river and across. The far hills are beginning to fade into the gray of evening, for the sun has set. One hardly realizes when this happens in this thick air of stormy June; but the sky glows with a warm light which is reflected in the expanse of water, so smooth that only the edges of the reflections are quivering with the motion of tiny ripples. The thrush, whose contemplative song all through the day has foretold this calm of evening, is silent now, and only the peewee carries on, his timid whistle rising and expanding to heights never dreamed of, as if he felt in the evening quiet that he was alone in the world. What is the meaning of this burst of ecstasy before nightfall? Is it to prophesy the rising of the sun after night has passed? Crickets chirp faintly and a bullfrog down in the creek strums a tentative chord. This day is over. *1965*

June 8 I have more to do than any man I know, more than I want to do, yet idle people often keep me from it and then they think I am always as unoccupied as I am when they see me. *1960*

These are sultry June days, still hazy, a pale sun burning through the mist, the soft clouds barely visible in the gray, blue sky. . . . Looking up the river I saw a bolt of lightning, an arrow from the sky that pierced the earth. *1963*

June 9 I will never cease to marvel at the different worlds people live in, yet they share some common interest and activity. . . . I want to ask people, why are you so indifferent to the beauty of this earth on which you live? They seem to live in a cellar—a luxurious, heated, air-conditioned one. *1961*

I do not remember such long sunny days, such wonderful nights and mornings. I am awake always, I feel. *1963*

The Maryland yellow throat has been singing sweetly by the river these days. How plainly the children's voices sound from across the river. *1963*

This day was given to the garden, except for the first half of the afternoon, when I was at the service of the piano tuner, who arrived on the other shore just as we began to eat dinner. He was a blind man, young. His wife had driven the car and she waited in it, fearing to cross the river. I admired the way the man conducted himself, requiring less help than many a seeing person, stepping out boldly on the rough way, in and out of the boat, uphill and down. He asked me to look at something. I had to get my glasses and a flashlight, both of which nuisances he's free from. *1965*

I would write only about the weather, or I would write nothing at all, rather than contrive a string of words that expressed no deep feeling, clever and literary as they might be. *1966*

June 10 Hot summer weather. The sun burns and the sand bottom is almost too hot for my bare feet. The last few days we have had our bath on the river bank in a bucket under the tree, then a plunge in the river. Each day leads up to this and after it, declines. It is like a change of seasons. *1954*

When I look up from the water at the green hills radiant in the sun I feel the remoteness of this place, its farawayness, as if I had just come here. This feeling is lost or dulled by daily living. Perhaps it is the new viewpoint, from a new element. *1954*

June 11 The smoked gar was delicious, as was the smoked eel caught Sunday. *1962*

Painting is much on my mind. I seem not able to solve the problem which has baffled me all my life. How to express myself. To imitate nature, giving the illusion of light, air, form of things, texture, planes, movement—this is not enough, yet it is primal and essential. What gives grace to a picture? It is an unconscious reflection of the grace in an artist's mind. I have lost my innocence. Yet even in my early painting I was not satisfied. "This is not it," I said to myself, and began the unending search. At times I had glimpses of that for which I was searching, but I never achieved more than glimpses. Yet looking back I see it there, good stuff in spite of myself. *1964*

June 12 The wild creatures about us are clever and watchful, taking every opportunity to snatch some of our food. . . . We have no defense against the squirrel. . . . In the garden he tears open the young ears of corn, and this year, it must be him, he has dug up several knee high sunflower stalks. . . . The rabbit nibbles in our garden, tasting everything. . . . Soy beans are the rabbit's very favorite, and he will single them out in a bean patch. Other varmints are abroad at night, 'possums, coons, foxes, polecats. *1956*

I must continually set my life on its right course, from which it is so often deflected by trivial matters. Surely joy, like health, is the natural condition for living. *1962*

What a delight to body and soul are shade, breeze, water! Surely they are deluded people who choose air-conditioned interiors and iced drinks—and the work they perform is not as honorable or productive as my planting a few rows of popcorn and potatoes. *1964*

June 13 A hard day, a guest overnight, M. Beers (one of the best) and many others here today, 4 crossings of the river, 2 cleanings of fish, the strain of entertaining people on their own level; of understanding and appreciating them. . . . I wonder if other people put out as much as I do in entertaining guests, in entertaining me. *1954*

June 14 The summer tanager, cerulean warbler, Baltimore oriole and sycamore warbler are singing freely now. Saw what must have been a bittern fly out of the creek Sunday. *1961*

The stormy, muggy weather of June is here, the ground is moist; the lightning bugs rise from the grass in the twilight and make the early night merry with their flashing. *1964*

To live one's life with people who do not understand, or even suspect your cherished hopes and tendencies, your aspirations, faith, who are innately antagonistic, and yet to be friends with them and admire them, make them be friendly and admire you, though even for your minor qualities, or perhaps even for your pretenses made in their interest—yet perhaps everyone does this, your friends do it for you, and they too are lonely ones. *1961*

June 15 _____ _____ is one of the few persons with whom I am entirely myself. Not that he understands me, but I feel free to present myself to him just as I am, with no adjustments or one-sidedness for his benefit. *1962*

June 16 Friends? You could do as well with the first strangers you should meet. We become accustomed to certain people, and desiring the familiar, we call them friends. Everyone has about an equal amount of good and bad. Remarkable virtues are found where not expected, after some observation. But an outstanding person, above the average in his concepts, how rare one is. *1963*

June 17 Writing is like work which you can do sitting down; rowing a boat, for instance. Painting is a stand-up exercise, like walking; so is poetry and the creation of music. *1955*

The pattern of bird song varies almost from day to day, reflecting the movement and changes in the life of the birds. *1955*

I tackle the garden again, wet heavy ground, weeds and grass, struggling crops, bugs—but what a joy it is. *1961*

River rising slowly, very muddy, but with little drift. About 9 feet this AM. We watch it apprehensively, but I do not expect any flooding. Yet— *1961*

The golden water against the tropical green of the shores and hills—who would want clear water all the time? Only those who see the landscape in a personal, hygienic or sanitary light. True, the water might not be good to drink or wash yourself in, but that should not interfere with one's enjoyment of its color. One advantage of swift, muddy water with running drift is that it keeps the outboards, or most of them, on shore. *1961*

The _____ family camped below the creek for the last two nights, though they slept in the studio. Fishing on the bar, using the johnboat, causing the dogs to bark, they took over the whole place, and my thoughts and attention. I respect and admire them, regard them highly, love them, one might say. Our welcome and friendliness are sincere. Yet I wake in the night when they are here, and feel that all is not just right. *1964*

June 18 I still think of the sunset yesterday, the whole sky aflame, seen through the close, massive trees of the creek, whose quiet water reflected the sky. It was a pastoral scene, yet wild and uncouth. *1961*

The sun sinks in the hazy sky
Pale shapeless clouds of gray, the warm light is dull.
Below, the hill is a gray-blue wall,
The hill on which I have seen the trees of spring,
And the trees of winter against the snow.
(The snow revealing unsuspected paths and dark rocks.)
The gleam of the sky reflected on the river
Reveals its flowing, its swirls and shimmer.
On its far shore the leafy trees are solid masses
Fringed with pale green;
But the trees reflected in the water are dull gold.
One feels the plane of the river all the way across. *1961*

What greater joy is there than to refresh oneself after labor? To get hot and dusty, thirsty, hungry and weary, then, at the call of a sweet voice, to lay down my tools, go to the river to bathe and swim, enter the clean cool house, put on dry, light clothing and eat the good food we have gathered together. The greatest joy of all on these hot days is to drink cool, sweet water. Sometimes after working in the garden I go to the spring to drink from the gourd. . . . At the day's end, as the light fails, I wash my feet at the tap outside, and it is good. *1962*

June 19 This was a long day in the garden, but now the pressing work is done. This is the point at which reaction and discouragement set in, and one begins to plan the next year's garden. Yet on the whole the present garden is one of the best. *1963*

A fresh morning, breeze and sun. We did a washing. It is worth something just to spend a morning on the shady terrace, the wind in the trees overhead, the scattered bird calls—how well the two go together—the sunlight striking through the June foliage. *1964*

The river is in its Congo stage now, a muddy stream—or is it golden?—flowing between luxuriant green banks, blue shadows of morning near this shore. *1964*

There are many tribulations—potatoes rotting in the wet earth (because I watered the rows before the rain came) before they sprout, rabbits eating the peas, so many jobs to be finished or begun. Yet the carefree song of the tanager overhead, the sound of the wind, light on water, there is so much, infinitely much. *1964*

June 20 I like the continuity of writing a book. It is like a long journey, you have goals in mind, you reach and pass them, aim for some other point in the distance ahead, all of which is unknown, or vaguely known, as if learned from maps and descriptions of earlier travelers; yet when you see it, it is entirely strange and full of wonder. *1954*

The season wears on. Soon the last summer plantings, and the fall planting will be made; and the longest day is at hand. The sadness that this incurs is met by the remembrance of the lengthening days early in the winter. There are no definite seasons. *1961*

Typical Sunday visitors today. . . . Received $90 for paintings sold, ten more for another when it is framed and delivered. Two small paintings, less than a square foot, one medium size (for me) of the creek mouth in high water, painted in oil several years ago, one of the *Robert P. Gillham,* recent, a small one of the bar, trees and hills across the river. Five frames to make. These people, all different, none of them knowing, are my best critics. They will have only a good picture. If they did not like my work, I would be disappointed and unsure. Yet I keep trying to break away and do something that would be more adventurous, more satisfying to me, pleasing perhaps to artists and critics. The best things I've done, however, can be understood and enjoyed by everyone. *1965*

June 21 Caught 2 nice catfish today, on doughballs. It is reassuring to know that they still live in the river. *1965*

June 22 The canoe makes a good fishing boat, if handled carefully. It is a delight, lost during our shantyboating, to handle a canoe again. It makes us Indian. *1952*

I heard in the early night a rush of the dogs, a fierce, brief squealing. This morning there was a dead fox in the garden. I wonder how the dogs ever caught such a light, long-legged animal. *1953*

The garden wilts under the burning sun. *1953*

Two days and nights of cool, east-wind weather, sky very clear and cloudless, air dry. The sun is hot, but with the fresh air stirring, it is pleasant to work out in the sun. When it becomes too bright and hot, I go down to the dark cool spring, have a fresh drink and enjoy the shade, looking up through the sun-shafted trees in whose tops the wind rustles, listening to the Maryland yellow throat and the redstart, hooded warbler. *1963*

Yesterday in Louisville, leaving here at 6 AM, arriving at the television studio before 8 o'clock. (We were expected at 8:30.) The whole affair was amusing, unbelievable if looked at with a clear mind, and rather dull. How commonplace and uninspired, on as low a level as the spirit of the viewers and listeners, who expect little more than noise and motion. Most of them want no more than that. We read some Epictetus while waiting. That was clear-headed, terse and far-seeing. Home in mid-afternoon. *1963*

June 23 Violent storm all last night, heavy rain straight down, continuous thunder and lightning. Creek running far out into river, which rose 4 feet overnight. Heavy drift. . . . The johnboat was nearly submerged. One oar lost, it floated into the torrent from the creek and shot down stream. *1960*

No matter what a man does, if he does it impelled by a principle in which he believes strongly enough to make sacrifices for it, particularly in the way of adverse criticism of society, family or friends, I respect him. *1962*

A swim in the darkness was balm. What a difference it makes

not to be encumbered with the least shred of clothing. *1962*

These are hot, muggy days, yet this morning a fine breeze was blowing, and this evening is just right. . . . Yesterday morning and this one I sat on the shady terrace shelling peas, for canning, a pleasant way to spend the morning. Some painting in the afternoon and a late go in the garden. Fine thrush song about the house. Now is my struggle with the weeds and grass. *1964*

Heard today the first cicada, quite faint, as if its first attempt. Frogs every morning. Where are they? Not far. They are the voice of summer. *1964*

June 24 Today all time and energy aimed at receiving guests from the city and entertaining. As they were leaving Roy Proffett came in to our dock in his bob-tailed outboard. He is a rare fellow, one of the old line. He knows his own worth, and ours, and we respect one another. *1961*

An expression like "as novel as green peas" from Thoreau's Journal—it would take paragraphs to explain its significance, and part of its meaning would still be doubtful. *1961*

June 25 We were in Fort Thomas the past week. . . . The Kentucky roads mean so much to me—every bush and tree, the barns and houses, shapes of hills, crops, the colors changing with the weather and season. This is an imperishable part of me. *1955*

I am rarely alone in the house, and the instant I am, a new feeling comes over everything, the house shrinks, the outside is nearer, new thoughts come to me. What if I were alone all the time? I shrink from the abyss, yet it offers glorious possibilities. *1961*

Some good hours in the garden, morning and PM, with a little painting time today. Perhaps the brief infrequent periods I have for painting are an advantage. Perhaps my work should be done quickly with great concentration, *raptus*. I have spoiled many a fine thing by not quite getting it at the first go, when I am working directly and intuitively; then coming back later to apply reason and judgment, experience. Perhaps there is still time. I feel that my confidence and strength have been restored. *1964*

June 26 This afternoon I am at the barn in the hollow, exploring its possibilities, tentatively, like a wren or a phoebe. *1952*

Our daily path is narrow. To leave it only a little makes the familiar landmarks seem part of a new country. Today I crossed the river in the outboard with the dogs, and instead of angling downstream toward Lee's landing, I headed downriver to pass close to a towboat that was coming up. Then I ran up along the other side all the way to E. O'Neal's landing and walked up to his house. Though I was never far off our usual course, the trip was something of an adventure. *1961*

I am disappointed in the painting I have done recently. It is trite and spiritless. Years ago I could do a good thing unconsciously. Now, it seems, I must build it all. *1962*

June 27 After a few days of hot dry weather and searing winds, the garden begins to wither, the spring ceases to flow, the birds become quiet. *1954*

The creek is perfect now, a strong stream of clear water, the rocks scoured clean by recent runouts, not a trace of green stuff in the water or bed. I bathed at the footbridge today, and feel clean in body and spirit. *1960*

June 28 All wilts in the hot sun, the panting dogs hunt for the coolest spot, leaving it soon for another. Yet they are always ready for a hunt. Sambo treed a small groundhog, barked wildly. Skipper joined and when I arrived they were frantically trying to reach the animal, 8 feet up in a small willow. After some consideration of the matter, I gave the tree a push, the groundhog fell. Sambo had it in his mouth when it hit the ground. He dashed off through the bushes and the clearing into the river where he swam with the groundhog in his mouth. He reached shore before I could head him off and I gave up. I hope they ate the animal, as we would have done. *1952*

There is always some thrilling occurrence or circumstance to write about, it is in my mind, I thought of it plainly when I was working out in the sun, or while playing Mozart and looking out on the familiar evening river, but these thoughts do not come into my pen when I take it up. What is the result, what is pressed out by all this beauty that surrounds me, the painting I do seems lifeless and pale, my written words are cold. *1963*

Yesterday morning I picked some black raspberries, dewberries and the first scattered blackberries on _____ ______'s place. It is not attractive, offers little for the painter. The fields along the road, worn out, are farmed by ______ for what they are worth, the rest of the place is left to weeds, brush and trees. The house is going to ruin. Sometimes nature seems to have no loveliness. Here nothing flourishes, there is no order, as in a forest. Perhaps after many years the soil will be brought back to produce healthy growth. Next to this farm, with a sharp line of division, is ______'s place, highly mechanized, treated with chemicals, cleaned up and trimmed. It is not attractive, either. Only the barn swallows. *1964*

Last night we drove to Bethlehem, Indiana, to see the showboat *Majestic,* now owned and operated by Indiana University. The play was in the old showboat tradition, but much better done, I thought. The *Majestic* is old, I remember attending a performance on it at Bethlehem possibly 30 years ago. Then it was towed by the gas sternwheeler *Attaboy,* the same boat that tows it now, minus the name. The showboat is the last remnant of what was once an important part of river life. The river is still the star performer. Last night as I looked across the water shimmering under a full moon at the gray hills, a navigation light across, beyond a resting sand digger, the massive sycamores lined along the gravel shore, I thought of nights in camp, and looked for a canoe pulled up on the beach. *1961*

The river and the valley seem larger at night, more withdrawn and part of a world in which we do not live by daylight. *1961*

I painted some in the afternoon. After the first hour's work, I thought it was a masterpiece, but next day it slipped away. I must break away from, go beyond the impressionistic concept, yet retain absolute reality, not illusion, perhaps, unless it can be suggested to a sufficient degree. It is hard now to leave the path I have followed for so long. *1964*

June 29 For me the river has returned to the primitive. The works of men hold no interest. The charm of the old days, the steamboats and old towns, has nearly disappeared. The river is part of the natural system, as the sunset and stars. *1953*

June 30 In these days of summer heat, how delightful the shade of trees, and the evening air, what a relief to swim in the cool water. *1961*

July

July 1 Visited with McMahans and McCords and Hammons. How good it is to leave the road and start toward the river. . . . Descending deeper into solitude we become ourselves again. *1952*

This evening a soft rain comes down from the gray sky, and sullen thunder rolls into the distance. My spirit drinks in the rain like the plants do. I will be watered to my roots. *1962*

Much goes into a day, and every day has its surprises, though perhaps only a groundhog which the dog treed, or the arrival at Lee's landing of two teen-agers who came to visit us. *1963*

If I could put into words what I see here, what I feel and think. The thoughts and feelings pass like the wind, only a small part of what I see is recorded. It is as if I were blind, and the world of sounds—meanwhile life slips away. Will there be no culmination, no climax? I am afraid not. *1964*

When I was in the river this evening, or late afternoon, I watch a towboat shoving its barges into the wind waves, which breaking sent spray over the head of the barges. The boat was moving downriver, between the line of hills, those on the west taking on the blue of evening, though their slopes exposed to the sun were still green. The far hills were solid blue and lighter. All this I have seen many times, many afternoons as they faded into evening. *1964*

July 2 I enjoy over and over again the repeated aspects of nature. This is the foundation of my life. *1963*

July 3 Sometimes I feel that my life's course is about run; again, I am sure that I will still plant many gardens. *1961*

Sometimes, almost always, the beginning of a painting, which no one sees but myself, is the best of all. Yet when I say to myself, this time I will stop there, the resulting picture is no good. I do not think that a good beginning is lost, though its freshness and novelty may fade, like that of the morning. *1961*

It is still cloudy this evening. The birds sing loudly, making the most of the fading light. *1964*

July 4 Yesterday the dogs killed a pole cat, in broad daylight, none seen here previously. Perhaps it came to the river from the dry hills. The list of wild animals contains pole cat, fox, groundhog, squirrel (red and gray), rabbit, chipmunk, mice (2 kinds), and mole. *1953*

After tracing the line (only 2 fish—a small catfish that got away and a small perch that had swallowed the hook), I noticed an outboard pulling into the bank below the bar and then some shots were fired. I rowed down and found two men on shore with guns, a young fellow in the boat. They said they were shooting crows and demonstrated for me their imitation crow call. Pleasant and friendly, they expected my approval as a matter of course. I wasn't very cordial, but invited them to visit us, after one asked if I lived in the house just above and painted pictures. *1961*

[Visitors:] With inward displeasure I showed them the available river picture with boats, which is what they wanted, but none pleased them. I do not speak of myself in this case, but the arrogance of unknowing people before a work of art is sinful. They should look at them all with humility, not condemn the ones they don't "like" as inferior, which is what they really mean. *1962*

July 5 Another hot day, and no shower of rain came from the scattered clouds. This is great weather, summer at its height. The frogs seem to rejoice at the coming of cool night. *1961*

A painting, to be good, must be done with dash and abandonment, even one which has meticulous detail. If one niggles over it, the result is dull and lifeless. It is only occasionally that one reaches the point where he paints at his best. Many circumstances must be just right for it. He could not stand it to paint this way all the time, and a level monotony of excellence would in time appear ordinary. *1961*

The night breeze nestles the leaves. What a caressing sound. *1961*

July 6 The songs of thrushes all about, filling that retired hollow with rare music. What atonement can one make when he mows a weed with a bird's nest and eggs in it? *1955*

July 7 Perhaps the feeling of hurry is generated in everyone by the machines they live with—can you be carried over the roads at 60 miles an hour, and see all day long a stream of machines moving at this rate, and keep your balance, and true relation with the natural system? Would a philosopher tolerate conditions under which this generation lives? When I am working in the garden with the gasoline engine buzzing away at its task of pumping water, I notice that I work under pressure, tersely. *1961*

No painting yesterday or today. When any unusual demand is made on my time, it is the painting that loses out. But it can survive anything. *1961*

The frogs seem happy, out there in the cool night. *1961*

In the evening a storm came out of the north, one that Homer or Virgil might describe. *1964*

After some mowing this morning I went up to the beehives, took out bucketfuls of honey, all I could carry down. . . . We never had so much honey. It is marvelous how the bees increase, and bring in such a wave of honey. *1964*

Sunday night and Monday night my studio was used as a shelter by passing canoeists. *1965*

July 8 Summer nights with frogs and lightning bugs. Soon the katydids will begin their death chant. *1964*

Each thread of our living has its special time of day. *1965*

July 9 We went to church today, to the Hanover Presbyterian, the reason—our guest, Nellie Wells. It is worth something to see a group of people doing nothing, not in a hurry, but relaxed and contemplative. It would be well if they were assembled for a worthier purpose. The religious part is tawdry and insincere. The preacher is shallow and evasive. If the congregation were not conditioned to the Christian doctrine, and tolerant, the preacher would have a task on his hands, to convince them of the validity— *1961*

I always figure that by July 4 the heaviest of the gardener's work is over, even though constant, almost daily work is still required and considerable planting remains. Yet he can slack off a little and think about other occupations that have been postponed until this happy time. Perhaps too his enthusiasm has been cooled by failures, drought, bugs and his own shortcomings and mistakes. His hopes are low, the unlimited possibilities of springtime are no longer before him. In mid-summer the garden is the hottest place of all. Yet he is cheered by the harvest, by the enjoyment of the good vegetables he has grown, by the thought of the long season still ahead; and all the tomatoes and okra that he can count on. It is a satisfied, relaxed time. If the days are hot, the mornings and evenings are delightful, the river water is warm, the air soft and balmy even when he takes his bath after dark. That is the best time, when solitude and privacy are possible on the open shore. The night sounds are joyous as bird song in the morning, and the lightning bugs are fantastic and unbelievable. *1966*

July 10 The river is muddy, a golden stream between green banks, a river of the tropics. *1953*

We took another load of canned stuff, blackberries, to the root cellar. It is unhandy enough, but the infrequent trips are always enjoyable, and there is something real about storing your winter's food in such a cave. *1953*

The river is in its most disagreeable state of an unchanging muddiness, very low. The shores, particularly ours and the bar, are covered with drift and the recent rises have covered what sand there is with several inches of mud. *1960*

The luxury and convenience of the houseboat that stopped here today was overpowering. So out of character with the river and its shores, that it would be impossible to feel you were on the river at all. *1962*

The afternoon was taken up by two pairs of visitors. . . . Vernon Robertson just back from Italy, where he is studying to be a Catholic priest, and a young couple just graduated from Hanover College, working with underprivileged (retarded?) children at Englishton. The boy will go to theological school in the fall. One question I could ask both—with what great and sincere conviction do you follow this path? *1964*

I went up the hill after breakfast, looked over the blackberry situation. They have been ripening for several days, fine blackberries in places, rather softened by the wet. Many vines have been lost. It is sad to walk where once they grew so tall and thick. I do not expect them ever to come back. *1965*

The garden means to us all our vegetables for the whole year, including potatoes, salad greens, herbs and goat food. All of it is grown without chemical fertilizers or sprays, without power tools. Thus it is a complex, laborious operation, extending through the year. Through the goats, we produce our own milk and meat. Fish from the river and our gleanings from fields and woods make up a good part of our food supply. It is quite flexible. If some item fails, we do without it until it becomes plentiful again; if it is abundant we eat it every day and can the surplus. Two crops which are important for us we do not raise—soybeans and wheat. These are so easy to get from farmers in our neighborhood, excellent wheat being given to us every harvest by our friend Chan Watson, that we receive them gladly, but not without a slight feeling of guilt, excusing ourselves by saying the time saved is applied to painting and writing. The fact that these two crops are fertilized with chemicals is more difficult to overlook and we may yet turn to producing our own cereals. *1966*

July 11 [Visitors:] A family of 5 people from Madison we had never seen. We wonder at first why they come, what they expect, what they want us to do, what they have to give. They talk little. In this case as the hours wore on they became part of the place and were reluctant to leave. *1954*

The reason I shun motors, machinery—I want the earth as a background to my living and thinking. These contraptions, everything about them—sight, sound, smell, operation—are from the city, and they destroy all that I cherish. They do save much labor and time. What do you do with the time and labor you save? *1963*

July 12 Last night, early and toward daybreak, the whip-poor-will sang close to the house. *1954*

So many people, of all ages and conditions, have an aversion to the expenditure of physical energy. This may be due to the widespread use of machines. Even the most trifling tasks are done by some sort of motor. Also I think many people are in such a low state of health that they have not the strength or energy—whatever is the cause, it is a sorrowful state of affairs. I could elaborate on this. *1962*

July 13 I wrote these words in large script across the top of the door on which I paint—"Paintings are not sold." To this will be added—"nor made to order." Perhaps this will forestall all questions which are difficult, complicated and painful for me to answer. *1963*

July 14 H. Boldery's father came down in a johnboat with Sid King and Webb's boy, seeking bait. The man is active, not old, seemingly. He has a gentle dignity which gives him the poise and gravity, and aura of wisdom, attributed to old people. Yet there is laughter in his voice. I understand what Powell meant by old-fashioned people. The open hospitality and generosity of Mr. Boldery, and the Hammons, their easy rhythm, their unworried good-humor, cannot be attained by the up-to-date progressive farmers, well-meaning as they are. *1953*

Yesterday after dinner and a brief siesta, I began work on an old painting, one that had been put aside unfinished for 3 or 4 weeks. It is strange what an inward satisfaction I get from just a little constructive work, a shape or color or bit of drawing that I know is right. Painting is the element without which my life is not complete. *1962*

I made the first blackberry expedition this morning. . . . It is disheartening to see the briars vanishing, the new ones diseased.

Wild blackberries will soon be unknown, only a memory that old people tell about. The prairie warbler sang for me, and the field sparrow. *1964*

River all clear again. Six catfish this morning, caught with cooked potato as bait. *1965*

July 15 In these days of machinery, tractors, power saws, outboard motors, automobiles, it may not always seem sensible to walk, row a boat, saw wood by hand and work a garden with a hoe. Sometimes the only reason seems to be the pleasure one gets out of so doing. It may not be economically sound—I haven't worked that out. But the idea of living simply by doing work by hand, by freeing oneself of modern mechanical conveniences, may not be as sound as once thought. The simplest way may be to work at some job, some routine portion of the complex economic structure of the world, live in the modern way in an apartment, say; then more time would be available for recreation or for whatever non-remunerative work one wanted to do. To go to the other extreme, and try to make or produce what you need—it would take all your time and strength to make a bare living. One would have to reduce his state to that of a wild animal. Not since man was nearly in that condition has he been self-supporting entirely. *1954*

In the evening a storm surrounded us, slow and sullen thunder in all directions in the dark sky. I hurried out to bait the line, and to move the fish box near shore, for the river was rising. Rain began to fall, and as I worked in the darkening twilight, poling the johnboat about, tieing things up, I was reminded of the old shantyboat days. With the storm, darkness and rising river came foreboding thoughts of disaster, gales and flood. Yet as the storm closed in on us and the rain poured down, the light of the sun shone through the thinning storm clouds, causing a warm, diffused glow, even though the rain was so thick that we could not see across the river. *1962*

At this point the gardener is likely to be discouraged. If it isn't a drought, a destructive storm comes along. While his back is turned, the weeds and bugs take over, or some mysterious wilting of peanuts or melons takes place. But the okra blooms and the tomatoes begin to ripen, promising a long and dependable harvest. *1966*

July 17 This morning I walked up the hills past R. Hamilton's empty house, past the old Willis place where part of a wall still stands. At G. Luckett's, Mrs. L. seemed to be waiting for me in the yard, and said that Graham was in the barn, where I passed a few words with him while he milked; then on to C. Watson's, more visiting and the sack of wheat which was the goal of this trip. Chan rode me and the dogs back to Gorman's from where I walked down, picking a few blackberries. They were not as ripe here as on the hill near Rand's which is open and sunny. The dogs made an adventure out of this trip and even to me it was something of that, for it is seldom that I go so far out of the regular path; it is like being a passenger, for all the details and execution are off my mind. My mind is open and relaxed. I enjoy fresh vision. Why do I not feel this way always? *1961*

Days shortening enough to notice in the evening; yet they are long and peaceful, sunny, ending in refreshing evening cool and dark, to be heard in the frogs and other strange insects clicking and droning, the silent flashing of fireflies. River in its best summer estate, now, clear and fresh. *1963*

July 18 Yesterday was a thoroughly rainy day, after a rainy night. The earth rejoices. *1953*

I am not a social person, I feel that I am always a party of one, on the outside. *1962*

July 20 This afternoon, after some painting (as yesterday, but for a very short time) I went up the north hill to my old berry patch, picked a quart or two from the dwindling briars. It is worth the climb on a sunny afternoon to come out of the trees and brush and see the rounded hilltop against the blue sky, the golden grass waving under the moving clouds, the hillside sprinkled with tiny cedars of bright green. *1963*

The river is warm and lifeless, no minnows. These are dog days, for sure. *1964*

I worked in the studio this afternoon, covering my tracks. A painting seldom progresses smoothly from beginning to end. If it does, it is either very good or worthless. In most there is a crisis somewhere along the way. The painting may not survive, or it may be born again. There may be several crises. Each painting is individual, unique in conception and execution. *1964*

July 21 I have been working in the earth and stone, digging, hauling, carrying, rolling the wheelbarrow, not to include well-drilling. What a satisfaction, what a joy to work so, if it is in the building for yourself, which you have planned and will use and enjoy. *1954*

The locust again today. Why do they not sing in earnest? *1961*

July 22 What a burden it is for me to have someone about all day, to talk to, listen to, appreciate, pay close attention. I am not used to it, I cannot take it lightly. Solitude is a blessing. *1954*

We had been practicing with Rand for the Hymn Sing this Sat. in Oldham County. Tomorrow we play Mozart with Dr. Bailey at Hanover. *1954*

I went up the hill for some blackberries, dead ripe now. Those too soft to put in the bucket are as sweet as blackberry jam, a concentrate or essence of blackberries, blackberries idealized and raised to a higher power. *1963*

Our recent guests, as they all do, disturbed the course of our living more than they realize. Not only the extra washing, the time taken from other activities, the interference with canning and garden schedules, but the emotional strain. The contact of other minds and ways—why is it always antagonistic? Because I stand alone? *1963*

July 23 I got myself so dirty this morning, from re-making the racks in the fish smoker and cleaning the stable, that I went into the river with a scrub-brush and soap, washed everything, including my spirits. How could one live without flowing water to carry away the dirt? *1961*

July 24 Those who say, What can I do?, must know the answer. It is, Give away all you have, and follow me. This means giving up conformity, the good opinion of the world, the easy reliance on custom. It means living imaginatively, aggressively, recklessly, enduring hardships to a degree. You must fail your family and friends, but in the end they will respect you. *1955*

______ ______ came across in his box of a boat, with visitors. He made a remark I often hear, and in every summer—"Here the summer has gone, and there hasn't been any summer." This puzzles me, for I think it has been summer, real summer, for a long time, with summer heat, summer storms, and a dry spell of four weeks. I think people live within their mental world, not in the actual one. *1961*

July 25 [After a trip to town:] There is much to recommend this modern world, it offers many advantages. Yet when we recrossed the river, and saw the untrammeled sky and the sweep of the hills, I thought, those people have none of this in their lives. How do they live without it? If I ever had to defend myself with a purpose, it would be to remind people of this earth on which they live, which they never see. *1962*

It grows dark after a long, hot, sunny day. The lightning bugs make streaks of yellow light against the darkening trees, a peewee sings his last notes for the day. A whip-poor-will has just sounded close by. The penned-up kids bleat for their mothers who have gone up the hill to sleep. Frogs across the creek, or rather toads, and I listen for the first katydids. I think I have never enjoyed summer more, or summer weather and summer work, summer heat and sweat and baths in the river. *1966*

July 27 Leon Barnes came down this morning with Joe, the Barnes' horse, and we hauled stone out of the creek. Pleasant work it was, good outdoor, country labor which I enjoyed much more than our hauling with the tractor recently. We got more done, and there was no feeling of strain or misuse of power and machinery. *1954*

A fair, hot day, sultry, with a morning fog. I was up in the first light, and after fishing and milking, went up the hill (to McCord's) for blackberries. Picked 12 quarts and was back in time to do some hoeing before dinner, also after dinner. Nice berries and good picking. In a retired spot where no one ever goes, I am at ease, a feeling I do not enjoy when out in the open, picking where the Gorman children might be. Some of the briars grow among small locust trees, and I pick over my head sometimes. Late in the afternoon I begin to reckon up the day, I give up much further accomplishment and figure what must be done before nightfall—the goats, fishing, bath, supper, and often occasional chores. . . . Time to play a little after supper, before fishing. Bath, or swim and bath together, had come first, then goats, then supper. The peewee still pipes. We may read a little before bed. Faint cheeps of katydid across the creek in the deep foliage where they are last heard in the fall. I suppose a life is like that—at last you cease to think of what you might still do, and wind up the chores before nightfall. Blessed is that man whose last days are serene and quiet. I have an idea that I will be busy until the last minute, as on some days, yet last night we sat in the evening listening to night sounds, watching the fireflies; then to bed. *1961*

July 28 The goats failed to come in last evening. I went up the north hill but that was a bad guess. I ran into them on the south hill under the cliff just about sunset. Following them down through the darkening woods, when I approached the river, the landscape in that direction was bathed in golden light, the trees at the edge of the river were dark and strong. It was a happy sight, reminding me of the old impressionists and the rivers of France; and of more than that, of visions they never saw nor dreamed of. Who can doubt a Higher Power, and immortality? This is what I live for. I have nothing else to say. Humanity means little. After dark I felt the soft air, saw the moon, as intimate as the hills, listened to the happy insects—and I too was happy. *1963*

July 29 The other day we were out in the johnboat when the current was running, and drifting down past our landing and clearing we felt the old rapture of drifting free with the current. We felt the smooth, silent motion of the river, which became a new creation different than we had seen from shore. We saw the familiar shore with new eyes, and it looked good to us. *1954*

We crossed the river late yesterday afternoon. . . . Some apples from the tree along the road above Harts Falls Creek. They are not good apples, misshapen, spotted and tasteless, but with Anna's patient whittling a good sauce comes from them. They are scorned by residents and passersby. Perhaps this is a survival of our shantyboat instincts. *1954*

Sometimes I feel that the whole world is against me, and I have not one friend. *1961*

As I picked the shining berries, wandering from bush to bush attracted by their red and black, I smelled the crushed pennyroyal and listened to the song of birds. The summer tanager has a nest near the berry patch, and the prairie warbler repeats his rising trill. Also the towhee, cardinal, chat, field and vesper sparrows, the goldfinch and white-eyed vireo flit past and in the distance contrasting notes of dove and jay. All this music and no man to hear it but myself in these brief moments. *1961*

July 30 We go through the routine of the day (canned tomatoes today), the chores, housework, gardening, fishing, tending the goats and all that, surrounded and bathed by this ever-changing atmosphere, by the fragrance of the earth, the evanescent colors of sky, water and hills—our actions, anyone's, seem insignificant. In such a field of action, how could one perform a base deed? *1962*

July 31 Newt was one of the first kids of Farny, with Brightness born April 12, 1958. He grew into a fine large buck, almost black with a Nubian nose and ears. He was usually gentle and tractable, and I could manage him even when the does were most attractive. Only once he reared and charged at me, and I had to be rough with him. Afterwards he often reared, and got between me and his favorite doe, but I could lead her away, and put him in his stall. The details of his death are too painful to write down. I miss him. He was a friend, and a noble one. *1960*

It is good to have Sunday afternoon over with, and to feel darkness and quiet settle over the river. *1960*

August

August 1 I spend much of my time at tedious chores, over to the spring, down to the river, to the garden, in and out the door. When I see and hear the work going on in the fields, great tasks accomplished in a day, I feel that I am not doing much; but what good is a barnful of baled hay? We still pick blackberries. *1953*

The other day, in the mid-afternoon quiet, Skipper barked "Snake" just outside the door. I looked out and saw a snake coiled in the dogs' drinking pan, completely immersed. I killed it with a hoe, ruining the pan. It was a pit viper, a copperhead, I think. . . . I wish I had been more deliberate about killing it. Perhaps it was blind; it acted so, as copperheads are said to be at a certain period. *1953*

I find that I have no part in the contemporary outlook. I have no interest in the interests of today—"electronics," "space," politics, high-speed jet planes, airplanes of any kind. I dislike automobiles, highways, television, and, I am afraid, modern art and music. Yet modern art, including writing, has much to recommend it. *1962*

August 2 The rain yesterday was a small cloudburst. It caused the heaviest runout in Buck Run that we have ever seen. We were reading inside, and, hearing an unusual noise, I looked out. The river about the bar was solid with drift. I went down to rescue the johnboat which was in a torrent of muddy water. Logs and branches of all sorts, stones and gravel were rolled out on the bar, and carried over our beach which was filled in for some distance. Perhaps an acre of driftwood lay motionless about the bar, which itself was covered with water pouring out of the creek. The rain did not last long, and the runout was soon over. *1954*

Caught a young 'possum in the trap last night, had it for

dinner. Very good. I will long remember his sad, submissive countenance, his long pointed face, and small black ears. *1956*

August 3 Last night I caught an eighteen pound yellow cat. It had swallowed a 1 pound catfish already hooked, and could neither get it down all the way nor get rid of it. This slowed him up so that I could get him in the boat. Otherwise the light tackle would not have held him. Yet he was still alive this morning when I dressed him for smoking. My previous record was 15 lb., also a yellow cat, caught last fall. *1965*

August 4 I enjoy unaccustomed leisure now, not leisure, for I am doing something every minute, but there is time for painting and playing every day, and for work other than gardening. *1962*

With these trends and the inclinations and desires of the young people I've met, there can never be another Harlan Hubbard. My position is defenseless, yet I am sure it is sound, and for me the only one. *1962*

I saw a great blue heron on the live-box this morning, a little green heron nearby. The big one was a warm gray of two tones. *1963*

August 5 One should be happy and faithful, even if he knew he were to die tomorrow. And who knows that he is not? *1961*

The past week, with intimate guests, three of them, seems now like a dream, and not a pleasant one. Why cannot I be at ease with people, be myself in their company, enjoy them? Perhaps I see them not as individuals, but as symbols. "Whoever is not with me is against me." I find no one who is with me. *1964*

August 6 I am tormented when visitors enter my studio, ask to see pictures, and then say, "What is the price of this one?" Yet they mean well. The picture is a production, a commodity, and the maker should have a fixed price for it. *1962*

August 7 Simplify? Our life is more complicated than if we lived in town. *1954*

This has been a good week, in the studio nearly every afternoon. I produce little, however, but little can be expected from an impossible situation. Then suddenly it will go well, and the problems vanish. They return again, however, and I have been seeking the answer for forty years. An answer would not be hard to produce, but reason cannot be trusted. *1965*

August 8 No rain Sunday, Monday or today, but much company. I give up all my time to them, also my workshop—and my thoughts. *1961*

Snapper told me yesterday evening that they needed my help with a groundhog and her language was very expressive. She led me up the hollow to where the road crosses the creek, a spot where they have treed 2 or 3 groundhogs. There was one up a small tree, which I cut and with some difficulty, because of other trees close by, lowered to the ground. The groundhog climbed another tree before the dogs realized what had happened. I climbed this tree, a small elm, and poked the little beast out of the tree. *1962*

August 10 The tragedy is—not to express yourself fully. Yet it is impossible. *1964*

August 12 I putter in the garden most of the morning, of every morning. There is always much undone, and will be to the end. *1962*

[After visitors:] Now we are alone again. I rise to the surface and see everything in its natural perspective. It is like waking from a troubled dream. *1963*

A hazy day, hot and sticky, becoming thicker until at evening the clouds made an early darkness. Then gentle rain began to fall on the dry and dusty earth. My mind clears at once and I am at rest, I see that my faults and weaknesses are not so important. I am still capable of a good deed. *1963*

Two more green herons flew out of the early morning fog, one alighted on the shallow water off the bar, the other flew farther down the shore. What graceful, impossible birds! *1963*

August 13 Rain all through the day, having begun in the night, not heavy at any time, with frequent pauses; yet a very wet day. With the two showers last week, the earth is wet and the plants happy. Now the katydids have begun their chant, though the rain still drips. They are in full vigor, not so easy to stop or discourage. Some fireflies gleam. The night is warm. *1966*

August 14 Sometimes through the day, never for a long period, I hear Bill Shadrick [across the river] leisurely pounding away at his new house—and I envy him; not just because he is building himself a new house—I envy his being able to construct a house to meet his needs and desires so simply and easily; and it will be a true shelter when finished. Most houses are so complex and artificial that they miss their true function. *1961*

August 15 This evening I launched the new minnow box. It is exciting to give any craft to the water, and no doubt some unexpected defects come to light in the most carefully planned. *1961*

[Visited by] a small motor house boat, some people (man, two women and boy and dog), on a cruise from Cincinnati, admirers of *Shantyboat,* who were making Payne Hollow one of their points of interest (the one farthest downstream). Mr. Stone asked for the honor of towing us across the river, which we granted him. They laid over nearby, visited with us most of the morning. I liked Mr. and Mrs. Stone—plain, uneducated (in the common sense), yet sound and well balanced. Some of his remarks reminded me of those of Epictetus we read yesterday. *1962*

The cool weather reminds us that warm summer is but a temporary state, like this fleeting life itself. Coldness is death, eternal. The warm spark of life glows briefly, we cherish it and are thankful. *1963*

A great blue heron flew into the top of a tall willow when I was in the water off the bar. The bird half-spread his wings to balance himself on the bending twig, craned his neck to inspect the strange animal in the water, and flew off with the usual arranging of neck and legs. It was in full sunlight, its gray in contrast to the green foliage. *1964*

August 16 Each morning after feeding and milking, the goats straggle off and vanish into the trees and bushes down the river shore. I wonder, do they long for the cool, sequestered places in the sandy shade, from which they look out onto the sunny river and contemplate their existence—or is it only leaves and weeds they are after, to fill their empty stomachs? *1961*

Launched the johnboat this morning, having pulled it out on the bank last Friday morning for its annual overhaul and creosoting. It is a rite which gives much satisfaction, and must be a good practice, for the boat is enjoying a long life—now in its thirteenth year. *1965*

August 17 This is a strange evening, after the thunderous afternoon (no rain here). Now the air is still and heavy, giving a misty appearance to the landscape. After dinner I fell into a sound sleep stretched out on my back on the workbench. When I awoke, it was to a new existence. I seemed to have infinite time and could do what I pleased. . . . *1961*

This is the season to undertake new work, to go travelling. What is the reality of time? I cannot comprehend it. Perhaps there is no such thing. And space. It is nothing but connected matter. *1961*

Anna canned the first tomatoes today, the beginning of a long task. The tomatoes are the best we've ever grown. What presumption—the tomatoes grew themselves. All we did was to make growth possible, and to start the plants. *1961*

August 18 The routine of our days is as regular as the course of the sun. It changes imperceptibly, as we adjust ourselves to the shortening days, react to the dry weather. Our work, mine especially, is affected by the slackened pace of growing things, by their ripening. *1962*

A party of 26 came down this PM in the Rodgers' outfit. Yesterday, barely after breakfast, 3 men and a boy walked down through the woods on the south hill—the Baptist preacher and 2 revivalists. At noon another party of 4—V. Robertson, sister and her 2 boys. Late in the afternoon about 8 Trimble County people of all ages stopped as they passed in their boat. They bring something, some of them, perhaps something tangible—a frozen chicken, a driftwood collage from V. Robertson, who is leaving for Rome to enter the Beda Pontifical Seminary for 3 or 4 years. Nearly all of them get into my studio and I drag out the same paintings shown to the last group—agony for me. Regardless of my sign["Paintings not for sale"], some ask to buy—more agony. *1963*

Today is the first day without callers for perhaps 10 consecutive days. *1964*

Reports from the temporary campers up the river, farm people, that they are catching many fish on their trotlines, do not disturb me at all. That I consider as a spiritual advancement. *1964*

August 19 Most men seem to live ineffectual, shiftless lives, wasting time, yet living in idleness. *1961*

I went up the hill in the morning, carrying 3 paintings—one for the Rodgers, one for a relative of theirs in Florida, one for Bro. Hall, one of the preachers who was down here Sat. The one destined to Florida is an oil on metal from the old days, a bare winter landscape under a heavy sky, a muddy road, a bare elm, a small creek flowing in 3 streams of muddy water, all carefully and smoothly done. To me it is very expressive and true, good painting. *1963*

August 20 No gleam of sun today, rain in the morning, this evening still cloudy, cooler, wind blowing down the river. One thinks of autumn, solitude. The green foliage seems out of time; yet the sun will shine and summer come back. *1961*

Suddenly the owls are heard—a screech owl early in the night, and last night a barred owl. *1965*

Every afternoon this week I have painted in the studio, beginning the afternoon with a short siesta, then a few minutes of doing nothing but sit, the only time in the day, then usually some little chore or a few minutes work at some job, then painting for the rest of the afternoon. I would ask for no more. *1965*

August 21 What a delightful place the barn is: the boat taking shape, boards and tools about, a workbench. At the far end, by the wide door which opens to a secluded dell, my easel and painting stuff; the bed platform in the center of the barn, where Skipper and the pups are in a little corral surrounded by boxes and cans, tools, nails, and the like; a corn planter and two-blade tractor plow. All this is small and scattered in the spacious enclosure. The floor is littered with old tobacco stems, sticks, dust and manure from horses which formerly sheltered there. . . . My easel is made of 3 displaced barn boards, weathered and warped, making a narrow wall on which I set my panel. A number of primed panels on the beams overhead. *1952*

Fort Thomas. In the city all week. Took Anna to the hospital on Monday and went there on Tuesday, Wednesday, Thursday, and Friday, spending part of the day with her. . . . To go to the city every day without an end in sight would be intolerable. I don't see how people can stand it, how the human race has adapted itself to such conditions. Yet the conditions are manmade, and most everyone seems to be content; at least they strive to be so. Nature is to most a form of sport, art or science. Yet I adapt myself to it [the city] to some extent. Now, Payne Hollow—living alone, away from roads and people, even houses and noise, nearly—it seems unreal and past. Of this, however, I do not think, do not let myself think. When we start back, a pressing eagerness and hurry to get there will rise in me. I am part of this world. I distinctly live a more natural life. The two overlap but they are separate in my mind. I have ceased to struggle to free myself of the world. I do many conventional things; rather, am carried along by them, as another rider in the stream of automobiles on the highway. The car means nothing to me, I would be deprived of it gladly. To be cut off from nature, the wilderness, outdoors, this would be intolerable. *1954*

This sudden changing back and forth from city to country brings them into sharp contrast. When I get back to the river I feel that I have come out from some dark interior place which was barren and cheerless. I am convinced that no one can be fully alive, mind and body, in the city. We may have ideas there, but not live convictions. *1956*

There is some unusual navigation on the river. Four white canoes, two boys in each, passed down on Sat. morning. The paddling was listless and inexperienced. One evening we saw a sort of raft, with a driftwood cabin and small outboard motor, slowly moving down along the other side, apparently 2 boys on board. A real shantyboat has not passed for a long time. Perhaps there are none left that could stand a voyage. More visitors yesterday, two young boys, folk singers, for dinner, a lady and her 12 year old daughter in the late PM. *1963*

August 22 Much as I admire the Christian principles and teaching and the people—and I think they are many—who follow them, for myself I require a more direct revelation, not one that must come through so many minds before it reaches mine. I must have a faith that I can see and hear, one that I can feel without thinking or even trying to put it into words. It is not for anyone else, it is a personal faith. The strange thing is that it leads to a conduct that I think could be called Christian. *1959*

Yesterday I went across the river with a few tools, intending to help Bill Shadrick on his new house. It looks not at all new, built of an odd assortment of weathered boards, but he did not welcome the idea. Nor me as a helper. He frankly told me he would rather work alone. Then he could adjust his pace to his strength, and rest when he wanted. If someone was helping him he would try to keep up, and wear himself out. I came home, having left my saw for him to use, and taking his to sharpen. I don't think he has used my saw, but has continued with the unhandy bucksaw. Today when I took the Pottses back, Bill was putting on the roof sheeting, the 2x4 rafters, nearly flat, already in place. He said he had gotten dizzy and nearly fallen off the roof. Why should he not let his neighbors help him? The spirit of independence burns fiercely in him. *1961*

August 23 These are the days of the locust. They begin before the morning dew and fog have disappeared and continue until dusk, overlapping the katydids. I bask in the sun, thinking of the chill weather to come, when warmth will not be free, but something that will be worked for. Perhaps an even colder time will come. *1959*

Tonight we baited the line from the canoe. To paddle a light, responsive canoe over the water gives a wildness and grace to the familiar shores. It is right with the setting sun. *1962*

As we went down to bait the line this evening, Anna saw a great blue heron fly up from the duck feed, a bucket of tomatoes. *1963*

When I go into the water, I am allied again to the earth and sky. These are supreme, and the occupations and cares of the day seem trivial. They are washed away. *1963*

August 24 Yesterday an expedition for peaches in the canoe; the first across the river to the familiar landing of 5 years ago. . . . It is good to get away, to see new shores, and feel the wildness and vacancy of the river. Our own landing was seen as part of the continuing shore. *1952*

I am never entirely myself unless alone; therefore, no one has ever known me. . . . Is the above true of everyone? I do not know. Yes, it must be true. *1959*

Five hours from the heart of the day with another person. Does he put out as much as I do? I don't think so. Nor does he bend himself as much to fit as I do. Yet the meeting is not entirely unprofitable to me. Every one contributes something, the amount depending on how honest they are in talking about themselves. Today it was a Hanover student. We paddled across in the little canoe. *1959*

Yesterday, the day before and today, visitors were here. . . . I wonder, do other people lead normal lives, spiritually and mentally, when I visit them? I feel as if bludgeoned and I am concerned lest the arduous trip here should not be worthwhile. What an effort I make to be cordial to them. *1961*

Where is the friend who will try to truly know me, who will study to learn and appreciate my virtues? *1961*

August 25 I have not for years enjoyed so much leisure as just now. Not since we came here to live, anyway. I work mornings in the garden, build fence, repair and improve; but none of it is urgent. Afternoons I retire to my shop, unless prevented by visitors or events, but this is not often. I have time to undertake jobs postponed for a long time, like the repair of the broken

Bruxelles violin. No doubt with the change of season, new work will take my attention. *1959*

After my friends are gone, I regret that I did not reveal to them my true thoughts; or my incompleteness or silence or my insincerity gave them a wrong impression of me and my ideas; also of my feeling toward them. *1961*

Now after sunset in the misty evening, the landscape subsides into flat tones, approaching the simplicity of night. *1961*

How sweet and tender the night sounds are. *1961*

August 26 At the core I am a misanthrope and unsocial. I feel this way when people come too close. *1961*

The world is made up of well-intentioned people, or they are to some extent; on the other hand, they are narrow and selfish, ignorant at higher levels, want 10 dollar "river scenes." I may have found a way to produce cheap pictures. Last week I made 5 paintings, about 12 x 15 or a little smaller, of the same "scene," each one representing a full afternoon's work. It was a significant experiment, and may open new fields. The "scene" was imaginary, picturesque and I suppose sentimental, but I want to be free of a definite visual concept, a certain terrain at a certain moment, and let the fancy wander. *1962*

I get out my pictures to show people time after time
The same old pictures, some new ones, too, not many
Because one does not paint that kind often
—Or any kind for that matter.
The people stare at the pictures,
Try to think of something nice to say.
Once in a while someone really likes the pictures,
Some of them, and they don't know what to say either.
Will anyone ever come who really sees them,
And likes them, and knows why?
It does not matter.
I will paint some more.
Perhaps I will transcend all these and paint
Some beyond the grasp of all who might see them. *1964*

August 27 I lay stone part of the morning and afternoon. How easy it is, how much of a pleasure to handle the clean, smoothed creek stone. And to raise out of the ground a straight, square, purposeful structure. *1954*

The shortening days are catching up on us. We must tighten up our schedule at the end of the day in order to have daylight for fishing. Soon it will be supper by candlelight. *1962*

It would be pleasant to wander along new shores at this season. One could almost live off the land—corn, pawpaws, stray apples, tomatoes, elderberries, pears, perhaps a melon. *1962*

August 28 Each day I see so much that is endearing. To list these trivial details would make a poem—the dirty, red corncobs in the barnyard about the crib, the flowers along the dusty roadside, a heavy bloom of trumpet vine now, the whistling of a band of jays, the crackling of the green herons who fish from the log, the whistle of a dove's wings. So much that is almost unnoticed, but which forms the substance of my life. *1955*

A shantyboat passed up the river last week, one I have seen before—a black hull with rake at one end only. It was towed by a johnboat at a fair rate. It drifted down last Monday. . . . A man (and wife) named something like Tharp, who makes a living gathering roots and herbs, goldenseal, ginseng and the like, which he sells in Louisville. *1955*

The rain ceases, the clouds lighten slowly. Then the sun gleams over the earth, through the windows into all dark corners. It darkens again, then more intervals of sun, as if it were sleepy and could not stay awake. The metal roof crackles as it expands in the warmth, and slowly the locusts begin their hot weather song. *1959*

I have been painting some the last few afternoons. It is strange after so many years that I should be so uncertain as to procedure and expected result. Each picture is an experiment and I never know how it will turn out. Many are failures. There must be some undefined conflict, I must be trying something impossible. In the end, a painting of mine cannot satisfy me unless it is an imitation of what I see, atmosphere, textures, perspective, proportion, color and form. Yet if I set out to do just this, the result is revolting to me. There must be some passion about it and an abstract structure of line, color and mass. The painting must be alive and moving. Yet if I try to achieve this primarily, the result is hideous to me. The two aspects must be achieved simultaneously, the one fostering the other. In trying to formulate what I see I unconsciously construct abstract form. After it is over, sometimes years after, I am amazed at what I have done unknowingly. This must be an act of the subconscious. *1959*

After drinking a quart of milk at supper, I usually have to get out of bed before morning. It is worthwhile to have something get you out to see the night. The deep night is not the same as the one you see at bedtime, or is it because you are half asleep, and the day has all faded out of you, that night seems so strange and the earth so unfamiliar? *1961*

August 29 I count 16 visitors here in the last 3 weeks, not counting local callers. I am never entirely myself when anyone else is here. It is like being ill, the mind is not whole. *1953*

One day this past week I made two little watercolors, like hundreds I have made before. At once I knew that this element had been lacking in my life the past weeks and months; at once all nature was in order, and my life was part of it, serene and confident. *1954*

The new car sits over in Freddie's yard, and is never in our thoughts. It is an excellent arrangement. If the car were here, it would intrude. . . . To drive to our door, that is unthinkable. It would change the nature of this place completely, as would electricity. Who can understand this? No one, from reason or imagination. And who has experienced this? It is very subtle and cannot be put into words very easily. Words fall into patterns, trite expressions, borrowed reasoning. Where can one read living truth? Only a few books have ever been written in this spirit. *1954*

I think if one would have nothing to do with engines and machinery, unless it were a steam engine, and if he could wear only rough, out-of-door clothing, he would stay out of trouble and have greater peace of mind. *1961*

Our visitors today. . . . A couple from Madison in a boat, prepared to see wonders. *1962*

It is certain that the natural flora as well as fauna has deteriorated. No doubt it is because man has disturbed the balance of nature. *1962*

August 30 Heavy showers yesterday evening and foliage is dripping this morning. All is hot and steamy in the bright sun. *1959*

I like to walk out on the bar; to see the tiny flowers blooming, the dry and bleached driftwood. *1963*

Much plagued with visitors the past five days, yet they are people we love. *1965*

I have been getting up before full daylight, have heard a distant whip-poor-will the last two mornings and this morning was surprised to hear a thrush. Now after dark a screech owl. *1966*

August 31 Sometimes the future looks dark. What comfort will a man have if nature loses its charm? *1962*

The conception of the world and our life on it—most people are dull and blind. Shall I say all people are? They share a common view. It is common to me, too, and talking with them I fall into their conception temporarily. That is why solitude is necessary. *1964*

Sometimes there seems to be little that is admirable about the human race. *1965*

Autumn

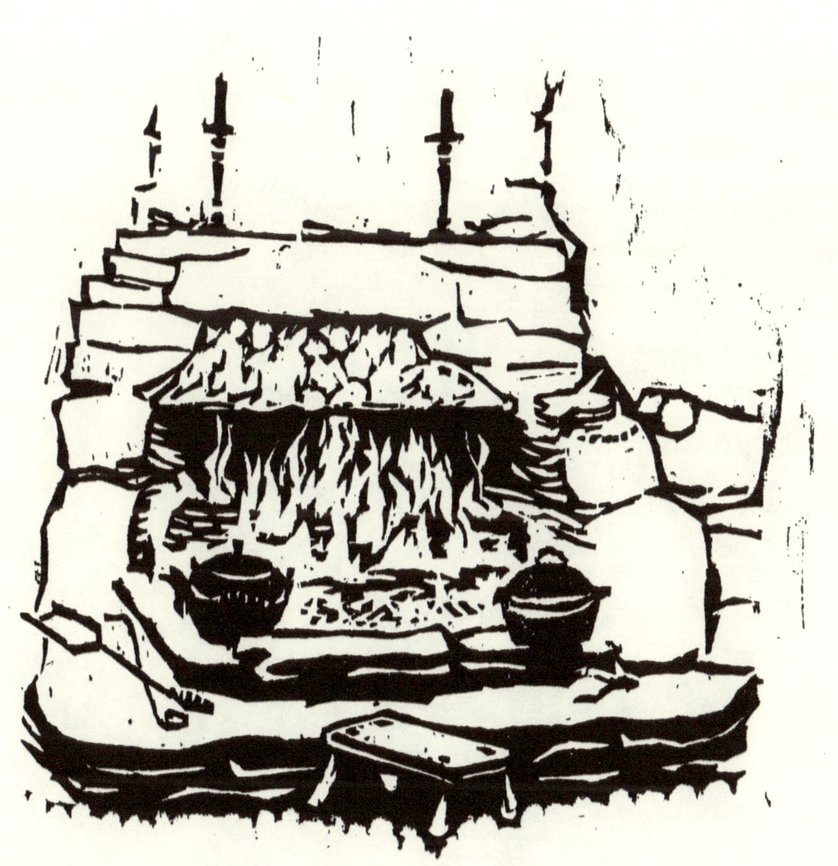

September

September 1 I have had considerable time of late for work—or puttering in my studio. I paint for consecutive days, or rather afternoons, with more enthusiasm than I've felt for years. I tell everyone I can about this, it seems a measure of success—to be able to give time freely to such an unprofitable pastime. Today, however, has been mostly taken up with other pursuits. This morning I helped Anna with canning tomatoes and some of her chores. After dinner several loose ends demanded attention, and then the dogs treed a groundhog which must be dressed and put in the spring. After that I began to cut dry sorghum heads, but that was stopped by a sudden shower. The goats must be let in, and at last I could enter my domain; to be called at once by a disturbance among the goats, which I did not hear, but Anna did. Betsy had tried to roust Farny out of a stall, and had hooked a horn under Farny's collar, choking her. Now I am back here, eyeing a thunderstorm, thinking the meat had better be brought in to a safe place. Here I go. *1959*

A strange bird voice sweetly singing outside the window as we played Mozart. *1961*

Johnboat launched this morning. How easy and swift it seems to run! Now we are ready. *1963*

September 2 Art is the last refuge. It need not be rationalized. What refuge do those have who are not sustained by the beauty of the earth? Art, with me, is only an expression of a love for beauty. *1962*

September 3 Our well gives us great satisfaction. It is a long way to go for water, but I enjoy the three trips a day. Each one is different, each day. The wind might be rushing through the tops of the cottonwoods far overhead, or I might look out from the deep shade over the sunny, motionless river. The view up to Plowhandle Point and Hanover is never the same. Each time I want to paint it again. *1953*

Boating elevates any work. Yesterday I rowed up along the shore, picking up pieces of board and some extra good firewood. *1957*

An east wind, according to the power plant stacks, though we did not feel it here and the river is unruffled. As often now, I remember some September days like this at Brent, an empty, brilliant sky, the earth gleaming as a desert, the water a deep blue. *1959*

The attendant difficulties bring out our isolation here. To us Payne Hollow is the center of the world, to all others it is on the farthest border. I feel quite cut off from the rest of the world. I am not affected by its forces. My one connection, the only one I feel except a liking for all people, is my painting. This is strange to say, considering that so few see any of my pictures, and no one is consciously moved by them. I put the pictures I am working on out of sight when Weston comes. *1959*

Yesterday Weston Powell came down on his tractor, spent the day with us; an adventure for him, and we both tried to make it meaningful for him. I rode back up the hill with him to cut some hickory saplings for handles, but could find none that would suit him. It is such an arduous trip by tractor, such straining, pitching and clanking. Yet the walking is so easy and quiet and unforced. *1959*

The sun rises and sets, and men go about their business, conscious of the difference between light and dark. But who is actually aware of the earth on which he lives? A man should be terror-struck in viewing the abyss, the void about him, and yet the sky is only a higher ceiling. More amazing is his indifference to the earth on which he lives a groveling life. Its radiant beauty should be an unending source of wonder and joy, yet most people live and die without noticing it. *1961*

The river and our spirits return to normal quiet after the turmoil of the holiday. *1963*

September 4 The present day warfare between groups of nations is unimportant. The real war is between man and nature. Like the other it is an undeclared war, without reason or goal. *1962*

September 5 Rain yesterday afternoon, beginning with a thunderstorm after a hot day, cloudy or misty. A strong wind with the rain; soon over, but more clouds came in from the west and it rained gently until dark. Afterwards a strong cool wind from NW. Our minds revived, we look ahead as if to continue a journey after a long idleness. New projects come to mind, the old ones seem to have reached the time for their fulfillment. *1953*

The sound of a cowbell across the river, the same one, but not heard recently. The baying of hounds, crickets and katydids; on a recent cool evening the katydids were silent; the wooden hooting of an owl. *1954*

The cutting of wood in summer is anti-seasonal. The woods are not inviting as in winter, for now one must wade through weeds and bush where it will be open in winter. Also, it is the hottest work, with little air stirring, the axe and saw are not kept sharp in summer, and there is much other work to do. In the simplicity of winter one can concentrate on woodcutting and enjoy it. Now it is a laborious chore. *1961*

September 6 An inside fire the past 3 evenings. A new season is begun. It is no longer the end of summer. To sit by a fire, to burn candles, such are the delights of the new season. *1953*

The katydids are silenced by the chill air. In place of their scraping is the ringing, ethereal sound of crickets. *1962*

There is no one with whom I would trade places, no part of anyone that I would accept in place of that part of myself. All is just right for me, even my technical abilities and physical makeup. *1964*

September 7 Yesterday late in the afternoon the dogs barked and ran to the river. I saw a skiff pulling into the bank rowed by an old man who turned out to be Jesse Powell, thin and gaunt, as diffident as ever. He spent the evening with us and slept in the shop, starting off early next morning, with his gun. He returned about 10 o'clock with one squirrel, the only one he had seen, which he gave to us. Then he left, rowing slowly up the river. No doubt he came to see us, and his beloved Payne Hollow, perhaps, as he said, for the last time. We were truly glad to see him. He has aged but is same as ever, with his sidelong glance and little smile, an expression which comes and goes in a flash. The river and the woods and the hills have meant much to Jesse. He truly loves them. *1961*

Anna's birthday. . . .The long-standing custom was observed again today and I took over the kitchen work—green corn and watermelon for breakfast, for dinner steamed squirrel, squash, okra and canned strawberries. Supper—this was Anna's—cottage cheese, tomatoes, boiled egg, lettuce salad, bread baked yesterday, and stewed elderberries. Again I was impressed with the order and smoothness with which Anna does this work day after day, the knowledge of detail and procedure she has command of. That cannot be learned off hand. Like all systems, however, hers has perhaps become inflexible and not experimental enough, nor alert enough for new possibilities. *1961*

Anna's birthday. . . .In honor of the day we had a picnic up on the rocky shore, paddling there in the canoe. I had already built a fire and in the coals were sweet potatoes and corn. After arriving we grilled catfish and groundhog. Also had tomatoes and peppers, watermelon and milk. No other method of cooking brings out such flavor. I swam in the river when the sun was warm. *1962*

Now is fair September, warm days, hot in the sun, cool nights. Katydids waning, crickets increasing. *1963*

September 8 Now we enter on the finest season of the year, when a long succession of fair days can be expected. The sun has lost its burning heat, it is pleasant warmth, even in the hottest middays. The air is clear and dry, too dry for things to grow, but the garden account is almost in. One feels that he stands at the entrance to some grand region, where all is new and changing. The time of growing is past, now is the flowering and harvest. *1955*

By this time my feet are tough as leather and I can walk anywhere barefoot. It is a rare privilege, one not understood by those who are always shod. They consider it foolish to risk injury, and that is always possible, but they do not know the joy of walking on the earth, feeling the changes of its texture, of wading in the water, of never thinking of what shoes to put on or making many changes during the day. *1955*

September 9 A bright memory of the past few days is of the huge flock of grackles on the stony bar. They lined the edge, in shallow water, drinking and bathing. Others pecked about the stones. A continual flight was kept up between the cottonwood, where the rest of the flock was, and the bar. The light sound of splashing water was as steady as rainfall. *1953*

The farmers are busy cutting tobacco, their wives picking tomatoes. I felt idle and useless. What is the meaning, or purpose, of all this observation? It can only be justified by some work which springs from it. I saw the sun shining on the green and golden earth, the blue sky. I saw weathered faces of men working in the fields, the smiling faces of women who looked up to recognize us. *1953*

Another hot, still day. Our operation this day was tomatoes. . . . The total was 11 quarts canned and 4 jars of juice. A long hot day for Anna, "working over a hot stove all day," as housewives used to complain. Few of them do that anymore. *1961*

A bucketful of catfish, one of which caught this morning weighed 15 pounds, the largest fish I have taken from the Ohio River. A yellow cat, it had swallowed a perch which was hooked on the line. On dressing the catfish I found the perch, 13 inches long, complete in the catfish's stomach. *1963*

The countryside grows less and less beautiful and interesting, less country. The old country houses are being replaced by modern boxes which do not fit in the landscape, and somehow the machine-grown crops have little character. The strain, unrest and dissatisfaction of the people shows up in the appearance of the countryside, though it would be difficult to prove this. Only when off the main roads, in poor land can one find real country, country houses and probably country people. Some true country people remain, even on Peck's Pike, but they are of the older generation. *1963*

It must be admitted that Trimble County is not a paradise for a landscape painter. It ranks below Campbell County. Yet there is no place anywhere that is as good as Payne Hollow, taken all in all. *1964*

September 10 I put out a new line this afternoon, sitting in the canoe on the still water, in the hot bright sun. Killdeers piped on the stony bar, jay and some cheeping birds in the woods. I looked up the slanting hillside, at the trees bending to the blue sky, the foliage coloring now, the varied texture of all kinds of trees, the color differences. The air has a quality peculiar to September. The water still warm enough for comfortable bathing. These still sunny days, why should one prepare for winter? This season will last, the revolution of the year is stopped. One relaxes in the sun. *1952*

Crossed [the river] after sunset for milk and eggs. The trip worthwhile for the sight of the river and hills as the day faded. How often have I seen the hills become solid blue in the shadow, the shoreline as it curved around the bend losing itself in the blue where hill and reflection were one. The opposing shore jutting out, an even wall of golden willows. The blue hills, becoming lighter, continued above the willows almost to the slopes on which the sun still shone. *1953*

I know when I am painting a good thing—it comes about when I am no longer painting with pigment and fashioning arbitrary forms, lines and colors, but instead I am working with the actual material I am making the picture of. The shapes come alive as I mold them and they glow in their own hues and textures. There is no thought of "form," "design," "arrangement." I know that when I paint on this level, the form will be perfect. *1961*

Yesterday morning I rowed across in a heavy fog, being out of sight of land for nearly half of the voyage. Made a landfall upstream of the point I had expected to reach. It chanced that a new dock had been built there since the last time I was on that shore, and for a few minutes I thought it was a strange shore, down the river in unknown territory perhaps. *1965*

As we sat on the terrace eating supper, the darkness falling fast, the katydids overhead and around began to sound, and the voice of a screech owl came from the near woods. What perfection of sound! *1965*

September 11 In desperation I caught a few grasshoppers for bait. It is remarkable how intimately acquainted one becomes with grasshoppers, for instance, or any item of the familiar environment, when the grasshoppers are to serve a practical purpose. *1961*

September 12 Sambo caught another groundhog this morning in the open woods near the root cellar. This while we were on our way to the cellar with the tomatoes canned yesterday. It was a half grown female; it is cooking now for our dinner. *1952*

When one wakes at night, not supported by the usual routine or familiar sights, he feels that considerable courage is required just to go on living in the face of the tremendous and terrible powers that surround him. No wonder that god was invented. Most support, however, comes from his fellow men, all are soothed and encouraged by this apparently invariable and eternal system of which the newspaper, radio and all associations of men are the voices. Without all this a man would be desperate indeed. *1963*

I bathed in the running creek this evening, at the upper footbridge. Who can afford unlimited, clear, pure water, running over your feet as you stand on a clean stone, carrying away all impurities? It is seldom that I can enjoy this luxury. It is more than that. I come away not only clean and refreshed, but purified in spirit. *1965*

Rain through the night, whenever I awoke, now gentle dripping, now rattling down, now scattered from the wet trees in a gust of wind. *1965*

September 13 A bright, cool day; the second day of a NW wind. Two days ago quite warm, but no rain at the change. The sun sets in a clear, almost colorless sky. The metallic whirring of crickets is the only evening sound, the chill air having silenced the katydids. The warmth of fire is to be sought. *1953*

We must not fall into clichés of thinking. We must face each day anew, and reexamine what we thought yesterday. Yet no one can be changed, in attitude, reactions, desires, any more than this physical makeup can be changed materially. *1953*

The Carolina wrens have hatched another brood, the third we have seen, this time under the eaves at the east corner of the house. *1961*

Two brief sessions in the studio, morning and afternoon. It is exciting, with boundless possibilities. *1962*

A warm evening, the insects are happy. Like them, we have forgotten the threat of winter contained in those cool nights. What if we had never experienced a winter, what would we think of these portents—the shortening days, the withering leaves, the harvest and death of the plants? *1962*

September 14 Painting these afternoons. How natural it comes, as part of the day, not disturbed by the work and chores, but fitting in as a related activity. *1963*

September 15 The sweet and innocent warble of the summer tanager, one of the charms of this hollow. *1955*

Today a stiff breeze, a brilliant sun; the evening so cool that no katydids are heard, the crickets sing alone. The cool weather opens new prospects. The fire in the fireplace brings woodcutting to mind. *1961*

The minds of other people, what a strange world is in each one, how I shrink from the revelation of it. What vast area of human experience is unknown to each one. How little do they suspect what is in my mind or the springs of my life. How could I live without my personal outlook and inspiration? *1961*

In this warm and serene weather I should be preparing for winter, but my nature must be like that of the crickets, who prefer to sing as long as they can. The summer routine goes on. . . . *1962*

September 16 I feel that I should give part of my work to the comfort and well being of some old persons, not in general, but for certain definite ones. It is the natural order. There are probably some not far off whom I could help by labor or companionship; yet I know of none who really need it. Perhaps Social Security has removed this duty from the individual. Sometimes in an indefinite, disinterested way, I wonder what will happen to me—when I get old and feeble. I know from past experience that when the time comes the way will be clear, and the problems I might ponder over now will not exist then. There must be unbroken rhythm. Old age is still beyond my conception, as it always has been. *1954*

A warm, still day, detailed reflections in the water, especially in the morning calm. Later, long narrow patches of light, where the breeze strikes. I work at stone laying. *1954*

Flowers are blooming everywhere now, but they do not receive the attention that spring flowers do. This cannot be from sentimental reasons, because the idea of a blossoming of the earth just before winter is as appealing as that which follows the period of cold. *1962*

Yesterday afternoon cleared and the night was fair with bright stars and moon; yet the morning was cloudy. We made the proposed excursion to Corn Creek bottom, however, with the outboard. A cold breakfast by a small fire on the stones at Preston Hollow. Corn Creek and below is almost strange country to us, we see it so seldom. The sweep of the hills upriver, very dark but fading into a misty distance, more wonderful than in fair weather. Landed once to get our bearings and farther down landed by good luck right at the Gene Davis farm. Our errand, long overdue, was to deliver a painting (of the river below Payne Landing with a distant steamboat) which Mrs. Davis had selected early in the summer. (Price $10.) They showed not the least surprise to see us on this unpromising morning. *1965*

September 17 We drove to Owen Hammon's, his new farm. . . . He is a magnanimous spirit. . . . I suppose Owen's farm would not rate high if land use and returns for labor and investment were considered. He, Norman and Catherine work hard there.

Yet their leisure, their easy-going ways, the fun they have, for they are born farmers and traders, could be achieved under no other way of life. Whose living is all efficiency and non-waste? *1953*

The day has been hot, but not uncomfortable. The sun is warm like a stove, which it is. I work out in the sun in the dry air, dry leaves sifting down. *1954*

The tangled remains of a garden are picturesque, with weeds in bloom and new ones coming up. Painting in the afternoon, then music, fishing, supper, all before the light faded. *1962*

September 18 A summer tanager burst into song, after clucking a few times. An indigo bunting sings now and then, I have not seen it, and I think it is a white-eyed vireo which sings like a catbird. These days are exciting for bird song. The last of the summer days, scattered and unexpected song of a reminiscent quality. *1954*

This was a sunny warm day. How good to be out, whatever is done, just to enjoy the sun's warmth, like an insect. This is a golden time. *1963*

Two good hours painting this afternoon. How well it goes sometimes. One thinks then that he has found the way, and it will be like that always; but painting is like walking the top of a fence, one soon falls to one side or the other. *1963*

Some painting in the afternoon. How exciting it can be and what new fields are waiting! *1964*

September 19 This morning I harvested some of the sorghum to feed the goats now, and pulled up part of a row of peanut vines. The sunflowers are all harvested. It is delightful to get all this in and dry, stored for winter. One feels truly wealthy. *1963*

September 21 How can this existence end, life in the open, skin bare to sun and wind, fresh vegetables and fruits in abundance, fresh milk? The season of cold, when we cut wood and tend fires through the short days and dig into the summer foods which we have prudently dried and preserved? . . . I feel an unaccountable surge of joy, even in the face of death and nothingness. *1961*

In the warm afternoon I rowed down to Preston Hollow against the wind and just about sailed back, landing here and there to pick up driftwood. *1962*

After the Saturday chores and some cutting of stovewood (locust, dry, from a very long tree lying at the creek mouth caught on the bar), I dug and washed peanuts. This is my number one occupation now. *1963*

September 22 Surely the abstract painters lose one of the greatest joys of painting or drawing—the mere representation of an object, if only a bar of soap. To study an object and reproduce the essence of its construction, proportion, action, color, texture—this is surely half of art, at least. *1961*

This evening is warmer, the crickets are in full voice, even a few katydids sounded faintly in the evening. Cloudy, as it was most of the day. A rather aimless day for me, chores and a mail trip in the morning, painting in the afternoon. How would it be to live with an abundance of leisure, with little work that was pressing, with some hours when you did not know just what you would do next? *1962*

I feel that my painting is progressing, new fields are opening, and it is a great adventure. *1962*

September 23 I saw the river last evening barred with wide bands of contrasting color, as it reflected the dark shore, or the clouds; or the clear sky above, as it was ruffled by the wind's path. *1952*

I hear the *Steve Click* coughing and puffing as she picks up the loaded sand barges. . . . To be pilot on the *Steve Click* would be pleasant work. *1961*

Up the hill for mail this AM and picked a few ears of corn from McCord's field. This can only be called stealing, even though I looked for ears that the cornpicker would miss. *1961*

Of all the people who visit us, from the farms and towns, college professors and students, some from Louisville who consider themselves wealthy, not one has a true understanding of why and how we live here, not one can see much good in my painting. Some like it for their own reasons, seeing it through their limitations, but they do not get the point of it. I suppose that true sympathy is not to be expected. Only a few are interested in painting, even fewer are moved by it—by mine, anyway. Yet I am moved by it, when painting, and long after, seeing an old picture of mine. *1963*

I feel more and more my estrangement from my fellow beings, not understanding them, but certain that they and I live in different worlds. How little people consciously reveal of themselves. They talk around the most important subjects, never mentioning or alluding to them, as if they did not exist. *1965*

I stopped work in time to have a swim while the sun was warm, a stiff wind blowing downstream. There was time for a little music, then Snapper came bouncing in to tell us she and the other dogs had treed a groundhog, and would I come at once to help them? I followed her along the wood path carrying an axe, she keeping within the range of my vision, eager as she was to rejoin the other dogs. I knew they were far off, for their furious barking when they first treed the animal could scarcely be heard. Now there was not a sound until I almost reached them, when Tray began to yelp, beside himself with excitement. This is a hard moment for me and I am always on the point of giving up the enterprise, yet I always carry it through if possible. This animal was high up in a slender ash tree in a thicket on a steep hillside. I could not shake it down, nor was the tree stout enough for me to climb, so I cut it. The groundhog was a large one, very fat as I discovered when cleaning it, a task which was finished by moonlight. *1966*

After the showery days the wind goes around into the west and northwest, clearing the air and sky. I take up my garden work again, for this is the time when I spend a few days or weeks harvesting and planting a cover crop. I am spurred on by the thought of frost, disturbed by it a little, not that I mind for myself or for the garden. It is the indecision—will it freeze this night or not? Shall I pick all the tomatoes green or ripe, the peppers, beans? Shall I try to protect them? Will it get cold enough to damage the celery? It is a relief when the frost finally puts an end to the tender crops, and to the questions which bother me. *1966*

In a few days the garden work will be finished, as nearly as it ever is. The springtime wave of enthusiasm and hope is spent. The cellar now gives one a feeling of richness and security, an abundance laid up against the coming time of cold, against misery and want. Innocent as a squirrel's hoard of nuts. *1966*

I have already sharpened my axes, neglected during the summer, and filed one of the big saws. It will be good to be cutting wood again. Such a simple task it is after the complexities of summer. Yet the garden is not forgotten. I have great plans for next year. *1966*

September 24 [After a trip to Fort Thomas and Cincinnati:] Driving down, I did not feel that I had reached home, or the place I aspired to, until the pavement was left, and Plowhandle Point and the wooded hills lay before us. Going to town, the feeling of country lasts until the final descent into the city, when something within me ceases to function. I am only half alive. . . . Surely life in town wears anyone down. A normal life could be lived only in such a place as this [Payne Hollow]. Here we see no geometric shapes, except our house and the plane of the river. No sounds but natural ones. *1953*

Not as many country people stop by as formerly. We enjoy and respect them, value them as special, which they are. The difference between town and country people is still there, though the leveling forces have taken some of the country out of farm people. *1961*

September 25 One morning last week, as we were eating breakfast on the terrace, we saw a red fox in the garden near the river, casually loping about until the dogs, who could hardly believe their eyes, took after him. The wild animal has a grace that no domestic one has. *1958*

September 26 Alone here, for a full day and parts of two days. When two people are together continuously, as Anna and I are, meeting no one else intimately or for very long, a separation is a serious action. For a short period, as this, the absence of the other is scarcely felt, for you know that she will be home again tomorrow. But I am sure that a long time of separation would be difficult to adjust to. It would mean a complete reorganization of your life. Even with my simplification of the housework, it takes considerable time, and I am taught how much Anna does, and how well and systematically she does it. *1962*

September 27 The summer birds vanish in almost a mysterious way. To think now of the song of the thrush, could it ever have been commonplace? *1961*

Weather unchanged. Men become uneasy, "We need rain," or "There is danger of fire." It is wonderful weather, we can be thankful for it and enjoy it. *1963*

Yesterday to Madison and Hanover, eating our picnic lunch on the lower end of the Madison waterfront with great pleasure. *1963*

At Hanover College yesterday it continues to puzzle me, the renown attached to us. A new professor meets us by accident. "Are you the Hubbards? I have wanted to meet you." I would like to ask him, "Why?", but he is friendly and interested, so we try to be likewise. We are less intimate with the college than we were, it is growing larger, more impersonal and business-like—a genteel factory. *1963*

I have faith in the young people of today, they seem a little different, their minds more opened, their vision wider than mine, perhaps. Few of them seem likely to be artists, for they are not mystics. *1963*

It is a joy to be out in the sun these days, to hear muted bird songs and see the blossoming of the year. *1963*

September 28 I take much time to do anything. This is partly because I try to do it well, to put something into it beyond the mere accomplishment of the object, something creative. Everything should be a work of art, to some degree. Also, in nearly everything I do, I leave the usual way, to try new ones. *1952*

September 29 When my mind is filled with people and events, trivial as they may be, I find that nature is shut off from me. I am close to it and observant of it only with a mind at rest, not distracted or absorbed by action. Even if one were a farmer or woodcutter, he might not truly see the earth on which he worked. Perhaps only an artist or a poet is in a frame of mind which allows a communion with the spirit of the earth. *1962*

Visitors yesterday and today. They take much time, I wonder if they and their contributions are worth it. Some are, I am sure. I suppose they may be called friends, yet I feel that I have no friend. *1963*

It seems my painting eye turns to the river in summer. Now the hills attract and I remember how beautiful they are in winter. *1963*

September 30 The voice of a single katydid, far off and faint, as if departing; it's at once a melancholy and a reassuring sound. It will come again with the dry summer's heat, in a swelling chorus; but before then—many rough days and a barren earth. *1954*

It is strange how all people carry their own world about with them, and impress it on others or keep it to themselves. They intend to perpetuate it as long as possible, and bolster it by every possible means, spending vast amounts of money to insure their health or property. This last is a deception. What in this life can be depended on? One can live only by faith. I was up in the moonlight this morning, and even though it was warm, I thought of the winter mornings when I've seen the coming day begin to lighten the east. *1961*

A beautiful day after the storm, sunny and quiet. . . . After dinner I spent time on the riverbank, set out the minnow trap, gathered a boatload of fuel, made a watercolor and later had a swim, which was skipped yesterday because of the cold dark wind. After the summer's use, not much good driftwood remains at the landing, and I work up and down the shore, gathering the best of it before the river rises and carries it away. *1963*

One may be outside for a long time, looking, listening, smelling, feeling. Go inside briefly, come out again, and the earth is strange, you are separated from it. The earth is ever new. *1964*

October

October 1 Last evening the newest of moons. *1962*

Another fine day. A very heavy fog this morning; I had to get my bearings before letting go of the trot line. However, the sun shone brightly, the fog soon disappeared and the air was warm in the sun, almost hot. This evening the chorus of crickets is full, even a katydid can be heard across the creek where they make a last stand. I have been out all day in the garden, on the riverbank, in the yard to work on the canoe. Anna heard geese this morning. No painting these days, but I make some small watercolors. I could spend the summer observing and painting at our landing place, the bar, trees, views across the river and up and down—enough for a lifetime. *1963*

October 2 Today we went to Madison and Trimble County. . . . The worthwhile minutes are the stops along the road—picnic at Milton landing near an old barn, a walk through the autumn woods to a pear tree, the meetings with people like Chan Watson, when the rind is removed and the true man revealed; also, sudden views of the river or across the country; or perhaps a few words like these are all that redeems the day, if that is accomplished. *1953*

No exertion will advance a man, or enable him to produce. He must be alert to know when he has advanced a step, or reached a new level, and he must know how to use his new power. One work of art which springs naturally into being is infinitely more than any number of forced productions. *1953*

A squirrel scolding and grumbling in a tree by the creek, fragment of an indigo's song, the titmice trying to get at the sunflowers protected by pieces of netting, the sun falling low. *1956*

A warm evening, after a day of strong south wind. The katydids make the most of it, but they are feeble. Now the sky is clear, the sunset glow spreads over the boundless sky, the wind is gone. It was a perfect day to wash our things, warm and pleasant on the terrace, where we had breakfast. I gather up loose ends preparing for rain, regardless of the fair weather. Then some visitors, and chores into the darkness. Some days are like that, others allow us to watch the sunset at our leisure. I suppose lives end that way, too, some busy and pressed until the last, others with a quiet time before night. That would be nice, but worst of all would be a lifetime of idleness or misspent activity. *1963*

October 3 I still see in my mind the view down the river from Hanover, Plowhandle Point and the opposite shore in shadow, the range of hills down toward Payne Hollow still shining with sunlight, a great golden thunderhead far eastward. *1953*

The companionship of people, their conversation, may have more value to me than I know of, to be revealed only when I might be entirely alone; but now it seems not worth the silence and solitude, the opportunity to carry on my own activities. *1961*

October 5 Yesterday the hot weather gave way to clouds and cooler air. Today is quiet and dark, with light showers of rain, a fall day. We turn indoors and inwards. *1953*

This morning made a trip to Eighteen Mile Island, which we circumnavigated, with E. Neville in his fast boat. I had not been down this stretch of the river from Wise's landing to the island since 1947, and was happy to see it again, to re-adjust myself to the landmarks. The Indiana north shore below Marble Hill, at Squaw Creek, is attractive to me. . . . I would like to make the trip by canoe in several days, exploring Squaw Creek, Westport, Patton's Creek and other places. It was novel to come upriver. The hills across from us here form a noble view. The speed of the boat does violence to the river, making the water a hard, corrugated surface, very unfriendly, confusing one in his bearings and snatching one away from what he is looking at. I did not feel that I had been out on the river in truth. *1962*

EN went from here in midafternoon or before, taking with

him two of my paintings—Shawneetown and one of the shantyboat-packet. I let go of Shawneetown with reluctance but it will be honored and well cared for. He intends to give it to Claire Porter, who has another painted on the voyage, of the shantyboat drifting. E. asked the price. I said, to his surprise, 25 dollars. I would not have sold it for 150, but since he would not understand my asking so much, I would have preferred giving it to him. He would not have understood that, either. *1962*

At this time of the year, as in the spring, planting, I give all of my time to the garden, harvesting and planting winter cover. *1965*

October 6 As I rowed back from the Indiana shore, the last rays of the sun made the autumn hill a dull red, which glowed against the heavy clouds in the east. Such pictures are seen, but not painted these days. The western sky was a band of golden color under the clouds. Against this the varied shapes of trees were distinct, the furry willows, the dense maples, the long top shoots of the cottonwoods with sparse leaves. *1953*

A pocket knife almost has a soul. *1954*

Heavy rains this morning, beginning before daylight. Creek running out strongly. We go about rainy day chores. I file the handsaws, a task which furnishes a satisfaction and a sense of virtue. *1955*

When I was working at the cover crop this morning a boat landed with a party of four good people, who took up the rest of the day. *1962*

Perhaps I could write a book telling about Payne Hollow and our living here from several differing viewpoints—that of our neighbors, of former inhabitants, of our visitors, of Hanover College and high school students, of the dogs, goats, and in the end something of our own ideas and evaluations, the whole permeated with the seasons, growing things, the landscape and the river. *1962*

We take little to give our friends on Peck's Pike, but they are generous toward us, offering whatever they have that we lack—apples, eggs, old newspapers, a piece of cake, and the annual 100 lbs. of wheat from Chan Watson. *1964*

October 7 More rain, very heavy early this morning. Now at noon a drizzle, colder. River has become muddy overnight, risen over bar and floated off the big log which was caught there in July. My spirits rise as I work in the wet and mud. The ease of summer and fair weather are gone, this will be hard and stern. . . . The changes come quickly and almost unperceived. We do not think of bathing or swimming now, and in just a few days my feet become somewhat tender and to go barefoot is as unusual as shoes were a short time ago. *1955*

This morning we finished the reading of Emerson's *Nature.* He expressed in uninspired ways, ideas I have had for myself. *1962*

People here yesterday. . . . They with a party of 5 altogether . . . staying quite a while. Another group (very numerous, with children) walked down the hill and still another (man, wife, 5 children, 3 of them their own). Saturday, 7 from Hanover College in 3 parties. . . . Sometimes I think we are imposed upon, but we ask for it, I suppose, and we get something out of it. No one can call us anti-social. *1963*

Yesterday we launched the johnboat first thing in the morning, having pulled it out for an annual overhaul on Sunday afternoon, Oct. 2. Thus it was on the bank for 3½ days, during which time I creosoted it heavily and caulked the seams. . . . All this improves my condition as well as the boat's. Now we are ready to face winter and high water. *1966*

Last night to the auditorium at Hanover College where I personally had a glimpse into hell where the demons played diabolical music. How sordid, hopeless it was, but they were defiant devils of amazing dexterity and rhythm. *1966*

October 8 Tonight the crickets are heard in chorus; there was not a sound of any creature last night. The sound of the crickets is one voice, one manifestation, one of the myriads of the spirit which hovers over the earth. *1953*

Last night to the hymn sing at Mt. Pleasant Methodist Church. . . . The goodness of these people, their well-meaning, their sincere love, this redeems them. How far superior they are to the religion they profess! *1954*

Warmer this evening, quite cloudy. The crickets resume their chirping, interrupted by the last cool nights. Not only is the volume of sound they make in close relation to temperature, the quality and character changes, too. Tonight their song is sustained, happy, confident. Last night one heard only a few spare chirps expressive of despair. *1964*

I don't know of anyone whose lives are closer to the changing seasons than ours. *1964*

The minds of people must be ghostly deserts, from certain glimpses one has inside of them. I suppose I would be shocked if I knew just what they saw in my paintings. *1964*

October 11 The farm woman snaps on the fluorescent light in her citified kitchen, all red and white and shiny. I miss the dingy, homey oil lamps, the smell of well water, the hand-me-down furniture, but the ladies cannot be blamed. *1952*

We stopped at Ollie S. Joyce's—surely a gentleman, a gentle man, of seeming broad humanity. *1953*

How many times have I climbed up into a pear tree, up into the sun and sky and wind, the round swollen fruit around me, green and gold and russet, hanging thick along the dark shiny limbs, Anna and old Jesse McMahan below, talking and admiring the pears, picking those they could reach, or the fallen ones. To go up a tree, particularly a fruit tree in the harvest, is to leave the world, as when one climbs a mountain or goes into a church. *1953*

Painted some in the afternoon. I feel I am doing the best work of my life. There should be no question about the rightness of painting steamboats, they can be a symbol as well as any other object, as well as the human figure or some animal. I have never felt so sure of myself in mind or matter. I am happy that I have never deviated, the long years bear their fruit. *1962*

These nights are of brilliant moonlight, a few katydids can still be heard when it first gets dark. One wants to enjoy every minute of these days. There may not be another summer. *1962*

October 12 Took a swim after sundown so I went in "bareskin." What a sensation, any rag of clothing spoils the best of it. *1961*

October 13 The serene weather continues. Perhaps it will last forever, having reached a state which is perfect for the life of man. *1953*

I went up to Donnie Barnes', since he had left a note in our mailbox about pears. His pears did not measure up to his good intentions. I gathered up 3 sacks of walnuts in his pasture, leaving them in his corncrib to call for another day. His place is as worn out and ramshackle as he is. Both in their prime were fine specimens of farm and farmer. I like the old man. He has a gallant spirit. He says he feels fine, much better, and expects continued improvement, yet he looks like walking death. This soil will not produce his like. *1953*

We are always under the shadow of death. Sometimes we forget. *1954*

The Akers [visited], and Gene had brought his new power saw to show it off, and to help me by cutting some wood and giving me firsthand experience. They are as efficient as a modern diesel towboat and as uninteresting to me. I can decide such matters, every matter, on an aesthetic basis. This applies to morals, religion and human conduct in general. What does not appeal to my imagination must be shunned. What a life one could lead, if he followed this principle in every act. *1963*

October 14 Living in one place offers no change of scenery, but it is satisfying to see in the changing seasons the same views of other years—the cluster of maples by the river, two trees leaning toward each other, their branches crossed like the fingers of two hands, still green, but paler already. They will become a light greenish gold, while the tall cottonwoods which rise on either side become yellow gold. *1954*

To those who live in cities, the weather is a minor incident. Living in the country, where you can see so much of it, where you are affected by it, with less protection against it, as from many buildings, so large that within them there is no weather, and especially in the country where you do not have the moral support of a multitude, who can talk down or outface any storm—the aspects and actions of the sky and the elements are awful, to be feared for their power. Mildness is a blessing. *1954*

The fair weather continues, quite warm all day. A visit this afternoon from Roy Proffett from Marble Hill. A genuine riverman, though he works as a painter at Hanover College and his houseboat is beached out. He says he is going to put a peaked roof over it. Yet he fishes, using nets in winter and some in summer, baiting them with old cheese he gets from Chicago. His grandfather Boyer was a pilot on the *White Dove,* built at Marble Hill, and ran in the local trade. Roy has much that is of value to me, he is a rare man. *1956*

The river has its fall look, blue water and light golden shores, the hills in flower. *1965*

October 15 Chimney Hollow is a lovely place, the scattered cedars becoming prominent among the thinning trees. Myrtle warblers and killdeers on the point. . . . Walked up the hill. . . . It is lovely to walk down the stony road, under the arch of the colored leaves, with wider glimpses of the blue river below. *1952*

The days continue a new and sunny perfection in weather. What climate could equal it, or what landscape could be more splendid? *1953*

Yesterday afternoon we launched the canoe, paddled up to Holderfield's landing, talking with Cleo Fresh on the way; visited the Bolderys. They were getting in corn, a good crop, as was Cleve Holderfield. Trout Bottom is a lovely place. It is good to see the wide expanse of the earth, its surface varied with trees and fields and slopes, houses and barns looking out here and there. All in the golden sunlight. *1953*

Old Mr. Boldery is another one of those mellow old men, serene and rich in experience, like the autumn landscape. Cleo is the clown, but one never knows his shrewdness or penetration. We ask each other questions which are freely answered. *1953*

An excursion to Hanover, Milton and Peck's Pike. . . . What complications and intricacies, what hard decisions, what tact, perseverance and understanding are required to get through the affairs of such a day. *1962*

October 16 It is quiet tonight, and for the first time we miss the crickets. I walked up for mail this morning, a muddy walk, even in rubber boots. In the big locust by the gap I heard a mockingbird singing, far off it seemed, but he was directly overhead, in the tree top, softly singing; to himself, surely, for the joy of it. *1954*

A boat from Louisville with six aboard to see us and our place, as if we were curiosities. Perhaps we are. Yet they are pleasant and sympathetic people, worthy people of high principles. One of them bought one of my paintings, because he liked it, I am sure. And yet— *1960*

In rowing to and from the fish line I often look at the bleached skeleton of a tree, quite large, with only part of the large branches left, like a strange white bone. A fine grass grows thickly around it, soft red and orange-green, its soft texture as well as color contrasting with the ivory tree. There is no comparable beauty in any dead animal, least of all in a man. What compensation of grace is there in dying? *1962*

I have nothing in my mind to write, no thoughts, no hopes, there is nothing I am looking forward to. *1964*

October 17 I rowed across the river this afternoon to glean corn from the field. . . . The cornpicker does a good job but there is always some left. It is pleasant there in the warm sun with a new view of familiar landmarks, the mind free, since eyes, hands and legs do the work. A mild form of excitement goes with the game when you come upon a huge golden ear out in the open, or spy a low hanging one in husks that the machine missed. Often even the most experienced gleaner is fooled by appearances and he grabs for an empty husk. *1960*

The *Avalon* went up this morning. Wretched as it is, this boat has true steamboat character—the way it moves through the water, its waves and wake, sounds, smells, and especially its sternwheel. *1961*

This continued fair, warm weather, and the ripening of the earth, from green summer to the varied and brilliant colors of autumn, affords a glimpse of life on a higher level than we know. It is marvelous that our daily lives go on amid this splendor. No heaven could be more fair. I find that my living is affected. I am more leisurely, my work is of little importance, it is aside from my chief concern. I wonder and enjoy as I go through the day. *1963*

Another fine day, another swim at sundown. I am busy today, but do nothing elevating. Yet it is good to be in the warm sun, to look through the woods, the eye resting on bright colors. This hillside, looking back as one crosses the river, is at its highest coloring. Could this brilliance have been expected, from the tarnished greens of late summer? It is the flowering of the year. *1964*

October 18 Have heard reports of a rise coming. Water from the spring now. The variation in the yearly pattern of weather, growth, rainfall, drought is part of the earth's cycle, like the revolution of the seasons. *1954*

Weather still uncertain. Cool, wind now from the NW. The clouds break away and fill again. The days bring scant result of any kind. People get between me and myself. *1955*

It is unusual in my case that I retain the dreams of youth. They seem more worthwhile and desirable and just as likely of attainment; but this last does not matter. *1963*

October 19 Hard wind from NW, ragged clouds and a dark sky. We brace ourselves for the first cold of the season. I wonder how important this wind is in the lives of other people. Perhaps most of them are so attentive to their business and affairs that they hardly notice the wind. *1960*

It is good to look across the river and see Lee's landing without the irritating signs of town people. Their discordant colors are like unpleasant noises. *1964*

October 20 My thumb was injured yesterday by a flying bit of steel from the hammer I was using. I can work as usual. I give daily thanks for my escape from serious injury. Sometimes it is by a hair, but I go on about my business. *1952*

This evening, before it was quite dark, I heard a single katydid across the creek, so faint that I might not have heard it had I not been there gathering wood. Perhaps this one is the last of the summer. *1962*

Sunday morning when our weekend neighbors from across

the river were here, in the midst of a general conversation Sarah called Anna aside to tell her something. Anna reported it to me later. Sarah had said goodbye, thanked us for being good neighbors. She expected to die before spring, and might not see us again. *1964*

I made two watercolors on the river today, a move toward regular painting. It is so easy not to do it—who cares?—and so much other work is at hand, and good pastime. *1965*

October 21 I walked part way up the hollow beyond the old barn, then up to the old road. . . . Good land along the ridge, but steep in the woods. No doubt the old fields were once farmed. One sees old fences, traces of roads, walled springs. I would like to take up some land like that, with an old house on it, and try to bring back productivity by organic methods, perhaps even using horses. What would be the point of it? Who cares for quality, or for the land? *1961*

Heard a faint katydid one evening this week, probably the last of the season. Leaves falling fast. Before the rain I got out the last of the potatoes, and put the last of the sorghum stalks in the loft. Cleaned the stable this morning. The summer's work is nearly finished. I turn toward painting again. *1965*

October 22 It is a different river, it has come alive, is going somewhere. *1954*

October 23 I saw a crow flying over the river quite far offshore approach the water close enough to pick up a small dead shad with its claws. There was no drift nearby. No inland crow could have done this so neatly. *1955*

It seems that the fall colors are holding back. The hills are quite green, the tawny cottonwoods by the shore a vivid contrast. How can I live on this earth as I do, such a lowly, circumscribed life? This sounds like Thoreau. *1955*

The extra work of butchering, the harvesting and planting of cover crop in the garden, and some days given to visitors have given some pressure to time, but now it is gone like the morning fog, and the earth, the river, the sun, assume their usual importance. *1961*

This PM I headed off the goats, or part of them, way up the hollow and followed them back to the gate. I like to watch them—who could enjoy the woods more? I wish I could get my living as directly and simply as they do. Theirs is an unhurried, peaceful existence, they are cared for and no effort or concern is required of them. *1961*

The cold returns like an old friend. He is rough and unmanageable but he brings many pleasures with him, like fires and wood-cutting. He simplifies and contracts our living, our circle of activity is more confined. Yet winter opens our outlook to its widest. It gives us energy and courage to take on again the high endeavors we have shirked through the sultry heat of summer. If one's spirits rise at the approach of winter, he is sound and in good health. *1962*

Today no one came, to our satisfaction. *1964*

When I am painting, or have painting on my mind, I see more, observe more carefully, am more sensitive to unusual effects. Perhaps, like the man who sees through his camera lens, I see through my pictures. *1964*

October 24 Yesterday I walked up the hill, Anna canning pears. The autumn colors change with the passing days, the oaks coloring deeply, other trees becoming bare. The landscape acquires an openness, new spaciousness. Houses and barns appear, unseen through the leafy summer. Many ducks; or are they coots? A creeper on the tree bark, strange passing bird songs, fragmentary. *1952*

A wren is caught in a mouse trap, which I, to my shame, carelessly set. His bill is broken. All life's tragedy is here. I wrung its neck, tossed it into the brush. There was a companion wren which had been much agitated, fluttering near the trapped bird. Now this one stays about, close to the dead bird, shrieking, if a wren can shriek, loudly uttering its trilling note, over and over. The wren flies away. A red-bellied woodpecker comes up chucking twice. He is not conscious of the wren's despair—I gather driftwood on the sunny shore, and am reassured. All is well. The cry of a seagull comes across the water. *1959*

October 25 Another golden day. We watch the progress of autumn from the river. The soft maples are the greenest trees now, but some of them are pale gold. The oaks are turning a strong vivid red. Other trees fading, the leaves falling. The bare trees of winter emerging; as definite an event as the first snowfall. *1952*

Juncos about. Always this early? The song sparrow the liveliest singer. Sometimes the cardinal sings, and on the hill I hear the mockingbird. *1952*

River falling, slowing up and starting to clear. Four good sized catfish this morning, on ten hooks, a short line along the willows baited with minnows. *1954*

A frosty morning, temp. below freezing. Bright sun in clear sky. As I think about it, the durability, almost permanence of a human life is impressive. How long a man lives, how many years even I can look back upon and remember clearly! *1960*

This morning a chickadee sung his four notes, and I heard a song sparrow this afternoon. The winter birds, including a creeper, are gathering about the house. *1962*

We have been quite overcome with visitors, 16 yesterday (3 for dinner) and 24 today, morning and afternoon, in 4 groups. The last party to walk down the hill met 2 others coming up. Taken individually, each one is worth talking to. We enjoyed especially today Robert Chandler, a country man of the old type, not old, and not countrified. *1964*

I seldom meet anyone whom I feel to be exceptional. They seem not to use their minds, nor do they develop their resources. All are content to, or at least they do, follow a pattern, like bees in a hive. *1964*

October 26 I dig carrots for supper, and think of the tiny carrot plants which we will tend in the bleak springtime. Now it seems doubtful that the courage, strength and faith will be found. The fearful and inexorable round of the seasons. It is no wonder that man fled from it, and set up an artificial system. Yet that is deadly. *1955*

This sunny evening, when we went out to bait the line, the

water was the deep heavy blue so characteristic of this season. *1955*

I wonder if anyone prepares for winter as elaborately as we do, storing food and building up our defenses against the cold? *1965*

October 27 A balmy day, a new moisture in the air; strong wind from the south, and great rollers in mid-river. The wind was down when I went out in the canoe at nightfall, the half moon luminous through the mist. While I baited a few hooks a fresh wind sprang up from the west. It was soon blowing a gale, the moon and the stars swept clear. *1952*

Good to smell the damp leaves, to see through the trees which have been so dense all summer. The walnut trees and buckeyes stand bare. What perfection. The leaves have been veiling the tree which now stands revealed. *1953*

The goats stayed out last night, which began with wind and showers. Perhaps they were sheltered and did not want to walk a long way through the wet, even for a dry bed. *1960*

Late this afternoon I made a long circuit through the woods. . . . The shaggy, overgrown fields, the scrubby woods, all in brilliant colors, the golden sunlight and the blue sky, what does it mean now, unless it is consolation for the passing of the summer, for the passing of life? Yet, how does it happen to mean that to me? It is not imagination, it is before the eyes of all. But who sees it? *1961*

I could write a book about the changes of weather and about my thoughts and experiences in gathering firewood. Why not? *1962*

This afternoon I noticed several cars parked at Lee's landing, perhaps 10 of them, quite unusual. Through binoculars a baptism in the river was revealed, and shouts could be heard. *1963*

It is good to have business on the far shore these days and make many trips across the river. The shores are spectacular. Today they were constantly changing in the cloud shadows. Most remarkable was the far shore above the landing, where each tree stands out as an individual, glowing in its own color against the blue hills. *1964*

October 29 The colors of sunlight and shadow are accented by the autumn colors, which appeared all of a sudden. The river hills are glorious. When I crossed near sunset to get the reinforcing rods, the downstream Indiana hills were in dark shadow, the sun was lighting up the Kentucky shore and hills in brilliant colors, beyond which lay a dark rainy sky. *1954*

It was good to get home last evening, wet and tired and hungry; to make lights and fire, have supper before the fireplace by candlelight, then some reading and bed. *1954*

A bleak day, with a cloudy sky and chill wind; yet I am so inwardly happy. . . . I am cheered by the broad view of the river through the opening trees. *1955*

October 30 There has never been a day in my life when I was not glad to be alive, when I did not feel that happiness and good far overbalanced misery and sorrow, when I was not sure of myself and my place on this earth. *1961*

I am reaching that blissful state of being caught up with the work and ready for the approaching season. I don't remember ever looking forward to winter with such eagerness. *1964*

October 31 He [Weston Powell] asked me if I had our winter wood in. There is a few days' supply cut, most of it in various piles outside. A large part of the wood we burn in the fireplace is from dead trees and fallen branches, often partly rotted. We burn all the small branches and twigs, with three different fires. I think that even if our winter's supply was cut and stored I would still go out first thing every morning with saw and axe. *1956*

Today, Hallowe'en, each of us made a jack-o-lantern. Anna makes much over every holiday, and tonight I am dressed like a scarecrow. Anna wears a striking blouse of orange and black with black slacks. She has made squash pudding for supper. *1961*

To be ready for a frost tonight, I moved more celery into the cellar and covered the rest. It is a good feeling to know the frost can do no more harm. We can enjoy it now. *1962*

November

November 1 A true November day, dark, chill and wet. Wind southerly, changing suddenly to NW, with heavy darkness. A strong gust and driving rain, obscuring Lee's valley. Then in the southwest the horizon began to clear. The wind and rain ceased. The band of clear brightness extended upward. I walked in the sodden woods, looking for walnuts. The strong, sober colors of the fading leaves, much greenness still, the straight trunks of the trees emerging, the skeleton of the woods now revealed. Both white and purple violets in bloom, a few. Successful living depends on continual adjustment to weather, time, to changing relations with neighbors. Woodcutting becomes more important and urgent, with a fire burning all day. How good to sit by the fire on such a day as this and how good to go out again in the wet. *1954*

I helped Weston Powell with the corn-shredding today, one of a crew of 9 or 10. There is much to observe and study, much to learn, much to admire and love, in them; much to be amused at. *1955*

Looked over the hill at the river and valley, bright with autumn and morning. The desire to paint again is stirred now and then. It could be on a higher level, with more definite aims and a sureness than ever before. *1955*

Perhaps the time will come when I will not be here in Payne Hollow, will not even be active and out of doors, so I will write about these days, about what now seems trivial doings, about the weather, the way the river looks under different skies, writing to myself changed and at a later time, trying to put a little of these days into words which may sometime mean more than they do now, and give an essence of the life that passed here—more concentrated and definite perhaps in a distance of time and space than I now feel. *1959*

This year the autumn colors burst forth suddenly from the dull, warm green of late summer, which threatened to pass quietly into the somber landscape of winter. This blaze of color, already dimmed by rain and wind, is like a late gleam of sunlight which for a brief time before nightfall transforms the dark clouds into warmth and lightness. *1959*

I helped Anna cut and peel pears for canning this morning. It is rare that she asks or lets me help in this way. The canning is a big job, running through all seasons, and Anna does it cheerfully and most extraordinarily well. *1961*

A brief spell of woodcutting down the shore. This I think is my favorite activity. *1961*

Painting is impossible sometimes. One wonders how it can ever be done, with so much to be overcome, with opposing factors that can't be reconciled. *1963*

I feel close to the season. *1963*

November 2 Unexpected guests yesterday afternoon. They are profitable, anyone is, for a short time. Taking the first two back across the river late in the afternoon, I was surprised to find two more waiting at the dock. Their signal had not been heard. *1959*

The effortless, slow sailing of a buzzard into the strong wind. *1959*

The day was redeemed somewhat by two watercolors, these few words, some woodcutting and other chores, but I am depressed to rock bottom. *1959*

You talk of God. Can you believe what you say? Only the savage had a true feeling of what God is. To the civilized man, God is only an idea, a product of the mind—God is not an ever-present reality. *1960*

At daybreak the reflections in the river were undisturbed by any wind. *1961*

The sky is clear of clouds tonight, full of bright stars. Last night the moon lighted the earth to its fullest power. It was perhaps one night past full moon and was quite high in the western sky at daybreak. I never saw a clearer air, not a trace of mist. The rising sun tipped the western hills and its red light slowly descended, a sharp line between light and shadow. *1963*

Two nights ago, while it was still warm, I heard geese, I remember now. *1963*

November 3 Heavy fog, most of it forming after daybreak. A sunny, still day followed. We did the washing, building a fire outside, eating breakfast and working on the terrace; very pleasant. This afternoon I gathered up leaves for the goats, filling all sacks except a few for walnuts. I raked the leaves from the creek bed, not far from its mouth, under the huge sycamores. In this dry season the leaves are not moist underneath. I used to fill the sacks and have them in the wheelbarrow with a rack, but find it handier to carry the sacks, two on each end of a carrying pole, like a Chinaman. *1964*

A wintry morning as ever I saw. About 3 inches of snow, but it looked as if much more had fallen. . . . The far hills looked pure white in the light of the rising sun, the sky was intensely blue, the air very clear. When I went out the path, I walked through a snowy grove that could have been the home of winter. *1966*

November 4 The sycamores stand out now, their white slender branches against the dark hills. The soft maples are conspicuous, too, their foliage a light yellow, delicate yet so thick that the trees seem solid against the airy woods. Along the river shore they stand out like round stones along a road. *1953*

When all my other work is in hand, I swing around naturally to painting. When I begin to paint again, I see everything as a painting, I see so much more. *1959*

I feel more and more that I am falling behind, or taking a different path from my fellows. Most likely, I am, or will be, regarded as old-fashioned and eccentric. *1962*

November 5 Looking through the trees toward the hill across the creek, the colors of the trees are much the same as in early spring, as I remember them from a painting never finished. The elms have the same rich brown as in spring, there is the same openness of the trees. Lacking, however, is the brilliant yellow green of spring. That of autumn is more cool and flat, of a color seen also in the spring. The great blue heron still here, and a kingfisher. *1954*

It is the time of the year when the cricket's song is in direct relation to the evening's temperature, not only in volume but in quality. On chilly nights only a few scattered faint chirps are heard in the early evening, and the night is still, a noticeable silence after the noisy darkness of summer. On a mild evening as this, a full joyous choir is heard, and the song is of contentment and hope. *1958*

I rowed across the river this afternoon after the clouds had broken up in the NW wind. A sharp contrast of sun and shadow in the glowing hills. It is unbelievable, that the earth is so fair. Who sees it? Who is moved by it? *1960*

I was taking a bushel of sweet potatoes and a cushaw to Fred O'Neal. All who saw them admired their size and I was proud of them. *1960*

Midafternoon, 4 adults, 3 boys came down the steep hill, coming from Manchester, Ohio to see us. Many people seek us out, not knowing what they came here for, nor do we; nor do we try to find out. We treat them all, different as they are, cordially and sincerely appreciate the honor they do us in coming. The glimpses we have into other people's lives are exciting, terrifying; with great courage and resignation most people live their lives, doing as well as they can, asking little. *1961*

The rain did not amount to much and had stopped at daybreak. One of the greatest pleasures is to wake and think daybreak at hand, then sleep a little, to waken again and find darkness still. You go through this several times, enjoying the sweetest sleep between the brief awakenings, not the dead sleep of the early night, until you are sure you have overslept; but when you get up, refreshed, the eastern sky is just beginning to lighten. *1962*

November 6 Woodcutting is becoming a part of the daily routine. *1962*

I suppose that the discipline of necessary work is good for us. What would it be like to get up in the morning and have nothing that needs doing? *1963*

It was a busy day for both of us, and in midafternoon the bell rang. We always have time to ferry guests across the river, and talk with them while here as if our time was free and unlimited. *1964*

November 7 I helped C. Hackett cut and shock the corn in the round bottom yesterday and today. Pleasant work, and you seem to accomplish much by your efforts. The scraggly field is shorn, the shocks are symmetrical and in rows. Little of this is done nowadays, however, with cornpickers and cutters. The dignity and grace of farming steadily vanishes. *1953*

The chunk of driftwood now burning on the fire I picked up at the water's edge at sunset. *1960*

The mild weather continues, no rain, no wind, but cloudy at times; but then the sun shines from a blue sky. *1965*

This is the age of gadgets. *1965*

Yesterday afternoon 5 boys from Hanover College visited us, all of them from Mr. Baker's Amer. Lit. class, with whom we will "discuss Thoreau" on Nov. 17. I admire these boys and am amused by them. How transparent they are, most of them. *1961*

Yesterday afternoon and this one today brought the usual run of visitors, some of them so worthwhile that their coming is an honor. *1964*

The hills began to show winter, and the red smoldering fire of the oaks is fading, their leaves falling. The hills as I cross the river are soft and delicate in texture and color. Can this be rough winter? *1964*

November 9 Yesterday I helped at corn shedding at W. Powell's. On such occasions I realize how seldom I am with a group of men. I do not mix well but singly I get along with each one. It is good to work out in the open fields. I could be busy at such work half of the time, if I wanted, and it would be the best way I know of to earn money. *1954*

A steady, cold wind from the NW this cloudy day, making it inspiring to work out in our open room, the windiest corner there is, I believe. The work goes slowly, handling and fitting the heavy, hard wood, none of it matching, much unhewn and unsawed. All this makes it the more satisfactory and rewarding to do, and makes carpentry a more elemental occupation. *1955*

A kingfisher has been flying up the creek, sounding his rattle. *1955*

In the afternoon all of us went after walnuts, along the road and up to Bill Gammons'. . . . Bill knew Payne Hollow intimately 60 years ago. If I had pictures in my mind such as he has, how different my conception would be. *1961*

This AM I cut wood, mostly on the Indiana shore, in the sun. That shore is as foreign to me as any distant one. The views are new. *1961*

It is so easy to break off the continuity of painting or writing. One wonders what he does with his time that is more important. *1962*

Fair and warm, after a heavy fog. Anna had much to do, after company yesterday, the regular Saturday cleaning and bread to bake. Also she must help me some with the canoe, sew a cloth cover on the roller I was to use for applying the resin, and in addition she remodelled my corduroys which were too tight, a chore which need not have been done today. *1963*

November 10 Today I took the last 5 small catfish out of the box, pulled the box out on the bank, put the minnow trap away; so fishing is over for this year. *1961*

Our visitor, Rafael Urbina. He landed below the bar in his yellow rubber raft, which I thought was something drifted in until I met him searching for drinking water. I brought him up to the house and after some persuasion he accepted our offer of dinner. He seemed tired, lonely, hungry and disappointed. His cheap sleeping bag was wet. It had taken him 11 days to get this far from Cincinnati. He said his home was New York City, did not give his age but I guess it wasn't much over 20 years. His outfit was wretched. One of the tiny aluminum oars having been lost, he had replaced it with a crude one he made of a small crooked branch, a piece of thin board and some string. We do not know what brought him here, what he was seeking. He talked of buying a "farm" in the "waste land," had expected to reach the Mississippi in 2 weeks and then soon be in New Orleans. I suppose most young men have such plans for their life and they experience the same disillusionment. *1965*

Got in some good licks on the new building, setting up heavy posts and timbers of oak and locust. It should last more than a lifetime, hardly necessary in this case, but I could have no peace of mind in a building I had put up in a flimsy manner. *1966*

November 11 Yesterday evening little Bimbo was missing. All the goats had gone up the hill, but Silver came down in alarm. We all looked, in the river lot, on the hill, in the garden. The goats had been nowhere else. Darkness fell—no Bimbo. I became afraid he was drowned in following Silver to the water, with the waves rolling in from the south wind. The night was mild and we gave up the search. This morning, going down to the stable in the early light, I saw Silver dash down to the fence behind the stable, and then I too, heard the faint cry—there was Bimbo, good as ever. *1959*

Approaching the river shore this morning I was surprised to see a solitary goose, a barnyard goose, I thought it must be. It was unalarmed. With dignity it took to the water, swam around the bar. A wild goose, according to markings. *1959*

The colors of autumn change their harmony. Now it is the red or golden green oaks, the pale yellow of the soft maple along the river banks. *1963*

To Madison, Milton and Hanover yesterday. At the college we heard a lecture by a woman on contemporary art. It was a sorry business, as was the jazz concert in the afternoon played by faculty members and students. Who could play that stuff with any dignity or joy? Must art reflect desperation, anguish? *1964*

November 12 Yesterday we went to Bill Gammons' farm for walnuts. Bill is an old timer and he lives way back a lane off the gravel road which leaves the Saluda Road. His house seems to be atop a hill and his farm seems high because just there the hollows drop sharply toward Saluda Creek. Bill Gammons is a solid person, hospitable, and pleasant to talk with. The walnuts were plentiful. *1960*

November 13 Guests dropped in yesterday and Saturday, down the hill, by boat and hailing us from the other side. We have to adapt ourselves to a variety of people—local boys and Hanover students, old men and women who knew Payne Hollow in their youth, children to whom the river bank and the wilderness mean adventure. Will that person ever come who will understand us, honor us for what we really are, and respect our way of life? Or, even more remote, will anyone see my paintings with a sympathetic eye and tell me they are as good as I think them? *1961*

Nearly everyone we talk to tells how busy they are. I never meet anyone who has as much to do as I have. It is because they are pushed that they think they are busy. When I consider all that I want to do, and the shortness of time left, I feel something of a panic, but what does it all amount to? Yet,— *1962*

Last Sunday we were visited by Leroy Boldery, who came from Madison in his small outboard. . . . Leroy has a bony, angular face which pleases me. He said he was born and raised in the old Stevenson house across the creek, and after looking over our place, of which he evidently had heard, he went to see his old homestead. *1963*

A new light has come into view, momentous as a new star, dim on top of the western ridge, a little south of Epperson's light on the river shore. This makes the new light come from the little cottage under the rounded silver poplar which was dying. I surmise the light belongs to old Rupert Moreland, who lived in this house previously, and until lately in the stone house at the top of Lee's hill, which place has been sold, we were informed. The little house has character, and when picking raspberries there, I thought it would be a nice place to live. *1964*

A fine starry night, bright with moonlight. A passing towboat insistently flashed its searchlight in our window at daybreak this morning. I was up to respond. *1964*

November 14 Scream of gulls today on the quiet river, ducks, and in the hollow an unknown bird song. *1954*

The everlasting pattern of weather. Yesterday a soft, sunny day, high waves rolling upstream when we crossed. In the night a shift to NW with rain, and the morning is cold and cheerless, still too dark to see without a light. *1959*

What are the minds of other people like? What an unknown region lies behind the familiar outside of even those we think we know. They smile and talk but never reveal themselves; nor do I, I suppose. Yet even this exterior of people has a definite, unchanging character, like a puppet. As to myself, I cannot see myself as I appear to others. To myself I am all inward; what I look like to others, how I speak and act, what impression I give, of all this I have no idea. *1959*

One step at a time we prepare for winter, abandoning one outpost after another, until only the central unit need be defended against the cold. Wood cutting thus far has been done along the shore in the stranded driftwood, but soon I will work in the woods. *1960*

At the end of some days, I am happy and content with myself, on others I feel disquiet. I think the difference is caused by my accomplishments during the day. It is always a successful day when I have done good painting. Yet a mishap like spilling some goat feed or hitting a stone with my sharp axe, may almost spoil an otherwise good day. *1961*

After the rain and wind gust of Friday night the landscape was transformed. Only a touch of bright color remained here and there, the hills were austere and dark. Summer was blown away like a shroud of dust, the earth was uncovered to the sky. *1965*

November 15 Today I took up the last fish line, turned loose the last of the minnows, pulled out the fish box, put the minnow trap and other gear away. The catfish, the larger ones first, seem to stop biting about this time, perhaps when the water drops below a certain temperature. I have caught a good many fish in the past eight months, no real large ones, but there were no long periods of poor fishing. Once in a while we can congratulate ourselves and feel confident. This was a warm day, no fires or jackets, wind southerly. The evening now is dark and gusty. A shantyboater would look to his moorings. *1960*

These gray days, the quietness of river and the somberness of the hills are natural to me. *1961*

Now I believe all the outside work, except woodcutting and raking up leaves for mulch, is done. This is part of the simplicity of winter. *1962*

Some painting, then unloaded the johnboat and went up the shore for some more pieces seen on the first trip. It was good to be out on the river alone, a corrective to yesterday, when a newspaper writer and photographer were here. Torment. That must be the last time. *1963*

November 16 Last evening a voice in the darkness, "Anybody home?" Anna said, "Powell," and so it was, with his mournful voice and seeming uncertainty. He said he wanted to walk up the shore early next morning to hunt ducks. Accordingly he slept, apparently a sound sleep, on the floor with Sambo and Skipper. We had breakfast by candlelight and he went out into the fog with his gun. *1952*

The winter landscape comes as an unremembered glory to the earth. The color becomes rich, the forms strong and clean, the contrasts sharp. *1952*

Leaves are gone from the trees now, and in the brilliant sunlight the earth looks scrubbed and brushed. *1961*

November 17 I saw juncos near the barn today and along the creek, that is, on both sides of the old chimney field, a favorite place for these birds. Their arrival is as important as that of the spring birds, and winter is a season to be welcomed as gladly as summer. It is more exciting. *1956*

Yesterday morning, returning from Hanover . . . I gathered walnuts from trees noticed along the river road, two sacks of second rate nuts. Then I stopped at a tree on the farm of Carl Turner, who had just passed me and issued the invitation. It was a tree we had noticed loaded with nuts earlier; they were of excellent quality and I picked up four large sackfuls, nearly the whole crop of that tree. We have already more than two bushels shelled and dried, three sacks of unhulled ones; now six more. I wonder if we will use them all. No one can say we do not take advantage of this wild crop, offered us freely as breadfruit and coconuts on a tropical island. *1959*

Sunday our visitor Ted Wadl asked particularly to see some of my paintings and I showed him a few, of steamboats and recent landscapes. It was the latter only that he was interested in and after looking intently he began to ask what this or that shape or color meant. I realized that it was an unfamiliar idiom to him—strange, too, for a symphony orchestra violist. He saw only the brush strokes, lines and colors, not what they were intended to represent; and I did not blame him. The common picture viewer has been educated up to French impressionism and perhaps to modern painting in which the formal element is more important than the pictorial or realistic. He reads the technique of these painters and sees what the abstract shapes and shorthand brush strokes mean. My own painting, meager as the output has been, has tended in this direction for a long time and it has been my conscious aim; but perhaps I have gone too far already, for myself and for those who expect a picture they can understand. Perhaps the bright colors and cleverness of the Frenchmen is not for me, and form in a picture is achieved not consciously or directly, but through working for realistic representation. Paint what I see, simply. When working for an abstract pattern I let truth take care of itself, knowing that I could never get far from the realism which was natural to me; but perhaps I had better strive for the essentials like correct proportion and drawing, perspective, the effect of atmosphere, textures and the like; the abstract design will grow unconsciously. *1959*

Last evening to [an art show in] Louisville through a drizzling rain, fog and darkness, which was relieved as we recrossed the river by the moon shining through the cloud layer. How ugly paintings can be, how frightful the human race. *1962*

November 18 When one works [building his house] as I do, alone, giving as little time to it as possible, and yet doing everything by hand and making almost no concessions, the result is crude and simple, though serviceable and attractive. Whatever aesthetic merit it has comes from the innate beauty of the raw material, and the feeling of handcraft; also, of course, from the taste and imagination and experience of the builder. When one hires the work done, if he has money enough, the product is carefully finished, meticulously planned, and artificial, impersonal, without the direct and obvious purpose of the other. *1953*

I made another expedition to the harvested cornfield on top of Lee's Hill, where I picked up 4 sacks of corn. That makes 9 sacks, 7 or 8 bushels, that we have gleaned there, worth say 8 dollars, a figure which does not convey the impression of waste that the careless harvesting does. I have been outdoors all day, cutting, boating in and wheeling firewood up from the riverbank this morning. That activity is hardly profitable, either; yet is good and satisfying. *1960*

These wet days have removed the leaves from the oaks, and the landscape has a wintry look. *1962*

I suppose that life under any circumstances would be pressing, but many people live with no concern about keeping warm and fed. It is all done for them. Here many tasks have to be attended to, they cannot be neglected—little ones that must be done daily, large ones, like butchering and gathering walnuts (on my mind now), that must be planned for. A day like this, seeing no one, and the Sunday break-down, one wonders what keeps life going. One could be excused for giving up, in the face of such immense dangers. *1962*

November 19 We awoke this morning to a snowy landscape, a wet, melting snow; yet some remains tonight. How true winter is. It is positive, adding its own touch to the earth I see, bringing something that no other season has. I think I hear a screech owl up the hollow. *1955*

In the afternoon Newt Perry and his son Norman came down to cut wood with Norman's chain saw. To see the saw sinking through the heavy logs as if they were made of butter, where I would have cut so laboriously and slowly with my hand saw—it was like driving a fast car over a highway instead of trudging along on foot; yet to me it seemed sacrilegious, criminal. It is depressing, however; I feel that all my efforts are a foolish gesture. I must think through this, work it out. *1960*

On last Friday afternoon we met with Mr. Baker's Amer. Lit. class [at Hanover College] in a discussion of Thoreau, which as always became a period of questions about us. Most of the students were attentive and curious though I don't think we made an impression on them, except perhaps for a few. *1961*

We crossed the river. . . . The countryside is lovely in the dark rich colors, and the river was unruffled by any breeze. *1962*

November 20 There is only one substitute for Nature—Art. It is a salvation, unfailing. It cancels the world. Man is an adaptable animal. Considering how unnatural his life is, what a remarkable fact that he has adjusted his living to it, gradually and over a long period. Yet I fall in with this life in the city, completely and without preparation. Perhaps this artificial way of living has become the natural way, and a "natural" life requires the adjustment. This civilized way is simpler—on the surface. *1954*

I rowed against the wind, helped by the current of the rising river, to Preston Hollow, where I made 3 small watercolors. Picked up a load of firewood on the way back, also brought home a mess of mustard greens I found growing in the cornfield at Preston Hollow. *1962*

As I write, the house trembles from the force of the wind. *1964*

November 21 Busy today strengthening our defenses against cold and wind. . . . While we were eating dinner, the Turner boys came up along the shore on horseback, hunting runaway cattle, they said, when they came in to warm themselves and eat something. *1964*

A visit this morning from a Jehovah's Witness preacher, the second time he has walked down here, followed by his young son, Sunday—dressed and carrying a bible. The man's name is Orba Boldery and he was raised at Payne's landing, in a two-room frame house made of driftwood boards, mostly. We walked up in that direction, and as he pointed it out, the site of the house was where we made maple syrup in 1947, finding then traces of human habitation which we thought were left by campers, but might have been remains of the old house. *1965*

November 22 The river this morning was of mirror-like smoothness, and all was flat tones of blue. Even the trees were subdued. *1955*

Yesterday as we were winding up the washing, I noticed a fancy houseboat stopped off our dock, a lady's voice called through a megaphone, on seeing me on the terrace, "Mr. Hubbard, will you autograph our copy of *Shantyboat?*" I had to row out to them because their boat could not run into shallow water, prevented from doing so by its deep draft. . . . They anchored, came ashore in the johnboat, had dinner with us. *1961*

This is Thanksgiving Day, and Anna kept up the tradition though our dinner was liver, fresh from the goat I butchered this morning. . . . As Anna said, every day is Thanksgiving. *1962*

November 23 No one thinks of dying when they are young. I believed that I was immortal until I was a grown man. Even now it does not seem possible, that I—that bundle of traits and habits shaped by nearly sixty years of living—shall ever cease to be active in this body, which itself is part of the I; but now I can at least see signs that I might die, that this body will cease to function and there will be no more I, that the white throated sparrow which I am hearing in this deserted hollow on this dark November day will not be heard by these ears, that the low clouds will roll over the river and land unseen by these eyes. *1959*

The drive along the river below Vevay is worth the trip, for the road is like it was 40 years ago, with the old houses. *1962*

Can anyone know your inmost self, even your closest friend? *1965*

I butchered a goat, beginning just before the sun went down. I perform the operation easily, but it does not get easier spiritually. *1965*

November 24 When I went out this morning under the stars I felt it was to be a warm, sunny day like spring; and it has been. We feasted on an enormous rooster, gift of the McMahans. I had gone up the hill the evening before, with some catfish steaks. A meager gift compared to the bird. *1955*

A remark of Newt Perry's—"Once a man, twice a child." A man of his age and experience, regardless of moral or mental qualities, will attain to dignity and wisdom. I wonder if his son will ever attain to such earth-sense. *1960*

November 25 How desperate the lives of men, often. Their pleasures are desperate. How little mirth and good cheer. They make me uneasy. *1963*

November 26 A clear night last. Calm about the house, with a light breeze down the hollow. Yet from the river the sound of breaking waves. I was up in the starlight, carried some wood, aided by the light of the late moon. Then went in, lit a lamp and wrote for half an hour. The recollection of the starlight, and of the writing, go through the day, make it worthwhile. *1956*

On this mild, still night, the crickets are sounding again, not chirping intermittently but whirring their soft continuous rattle, it seems far off. This night before moonrise and under a cloudy sky is as dark as it can be. Lights reflected in the river can be seen, but not the river. The weather is always an adventure. It is always new, and one cannot say to what extremes it will go. I would not want to know what the weather to come will be, more than I want to know the future course of my life. *1961*

November 27 This day began dark and warm, slowly became cooler and more light until this evening the sky is clear, a fresh breeze is blowing from NW. River shows some signs of rising, with some current and drift, only the top of the bar shows. The silhouette of the shore has changed, the river asserts itself. When will I get to painting again? *1961*

A fair night and morning, the moon bright. Before sunrise a fog rose on the river, the water remaining clear of fog off the bar for a while, but it too was shrouded, and then the hills. It lasted well through the morning. The evening is clear, no clouds or wind. The western sky is a flush of color which is reflected in the water, the trees, the bar and all this shore in sharp silhouette. Moon three quarters full rising over the eastern ridge. I could be happy enough just observing all this, day after day, as I go about my simple tasks. *1963*

November 28 River is rising a little and it has lost its summer clarity. I had to move the johnboat in toward the bank, move the outboard, the barrel and the canoe from their summer low-water position. This is exciting. *1964*

November 29 Heard a screech owl somewhere in the hollow this evening. What a lonely place this would be to a stranger at nightfall. *1955*

Yesterday we brought the Steinway grand [piano] down here. Day before W. Powell and I hauled it from Madison railroad station. The whole project required much strategy and coordination, and in the end, considerable lifting power. Eight of us to carry. . . . The little piano, which we so proudly installed last June, was hauled back up the hill. *1956*

Carl Turner is one of our favorite characters. A little old man, with a small head and features, his clothes always seeming too big for him. He was a riverman before he became a farmer, being a shipwright and pilot in the last days of packet boating. He worked on one boat that was built at Plowhandle Point. . . . A few years ago Turner borrowed our U.S.E.D. river book to refresh his memory of lights and landings in order to renew his pilot's license between Louisville and Richmond. This he accomplished, though the license is of no use to him. I suppose everyone can be excused for being sensitive about the river and boats. He went to some trouble to show me his adze, the one he used in working on steamboat hulls, and offered me the use of it. *1961*

The river in the sun yesterday, reflecting the blue sky, the sunny hills in their winter warmth and bareness. Later under the cloudy sky the reflections of the dark hills were blue and purple. I can still see the river beyond the stark black trees on the shore at Lee's landing, their wild upright lines against the formal planes of river and hills. *1962*

This afternoon W. Powell came down on his tractor, causing a revision of the afternoon's plans, to say the least. I rode up with him to make a telephone call. All such business is not for me, nor intimacy with anyone. I am myself only when cutting wood by the river, of which I did some as the sun went down. *1962*

Yesterday was a quiet sunny day. We had our Thanksgiving dinner on the tip of the bar, warm in the sun with light upstream breeze. A camp fire did not tempt us. *1963*

November 30 I sailed out for wood this PM, coasting the far shore downstream to a likely driftpile. Here I chopped, sawed and rummaged a boat load. . . . This is work on a small scale—trivial, yet how many people at their work, highly skilled and farsighted in their judgment, can feel the rightness that I do on the riverbank this gray November day? And the few lines and colors I put on paper perfectly express my feeling for this earth on which we live. How beautiful it is, how remote, how comforting! *1960*

Winter

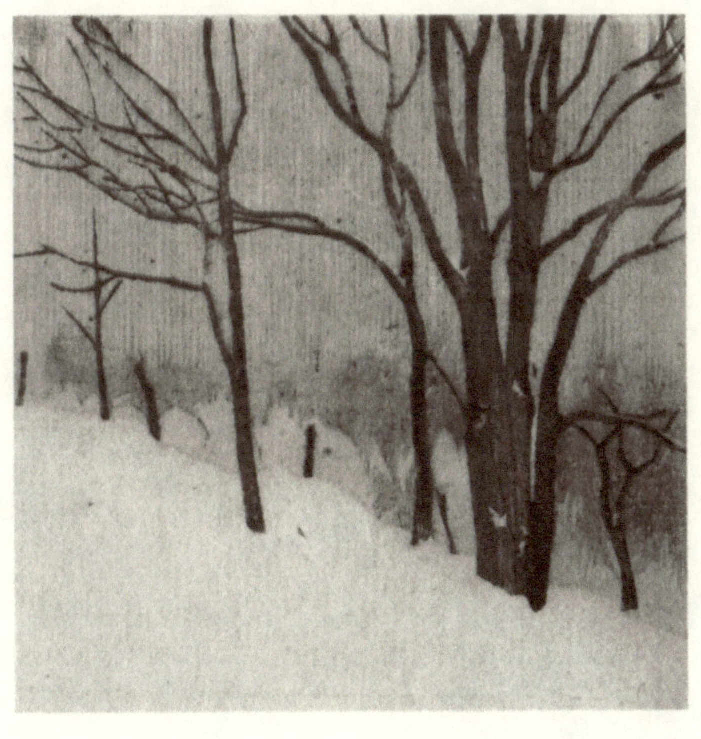

December

December 1 Fog this morning, and frostwork on the riverside trees, a brilliant spectacle when the sun broke through. *1965*

A wintry night, dark and sleety, a cold wind sweeping down the river. We are thankful for shelter and warmth and abundant food, warm clothing; yet all this alone could not give us much satisfaction or happiness. This comes from wood fires, from food almost as natural as wood burning, from the satisfaction of having cut your own wood, produced your own food, built a house just for ourselves. *1966*

December 2 Late in the afternoon I walked up the hill for mail, a wet walk. The course is so familiar, and restful, and the time of the walk is for contemplation and meditation or dreaming. Heard a robin again today. *1955*

I received a significant idea last evening as we read something about psychoanalysis and art, by Jung. Perhaps my tendency to the simple, natural way—wood fires, cutting my own fuel, raising or foraging for my own food, fishing, even the goats; also my distrust for the complicated roundabout way in which civilization gets the necessities of life—this feeling springs from a primitive instinct in the human race, an old experience which has faded away in civilized man, except in the subconscious. Then it may be that my gestures toward an old, forgotten way of life aroused a deep instinct. . . . *1958*

The goats have been coming in mornings for breakfast, then after a short rest in the stable they are off for the woods again. I think they spend the night on the cliffs to the south, perhaps under them to be warmer. They came in early this morning, announced by a faint tinkle of a bell from high up in the frosty twilight. The bell indicates not only their position on their course, but the nature of it. When the way is steep, there is a lively jingling as they come down with a rush. Then there is silence, when they stop to browse. As they thread their way along the creek bank and the river shore, the bell accompaniment is *andante piano*. *1962*

How rooted in the past I am! These young fellows [modern artists] trying to forge ahead, to do something living and contemporary, deserve much credit. Yet how much of their work is original, springing from within, and expressing something deeply felt? And who has done just what I am doing? At least, it is all I can do with honor and sincerity. What is there to do? What is required? Perhaps the Four Last Things still rule—death, judgment, heaven and hell. Only these are in force during life. *1963*

Pre-daybreak is a special time of day, having no connection with the rest of it. When I think of it when the sun is bright, it seems part of the night and my actions then might have been dreamed. *1965*

Much of my life is preparation for changing weather, colder or warmer, possible rain or fair weather. Cold or rain demand the most. In winter, if there is a chance of wet weather next day, I give extra time to getting in firewood. Even in summer the woodbox for the cookstove must be filled. This evening I had to get in some walnuts that were drying, clean the gutters, put a clean strainer cloth in the filter of the cistern, see that the cistern was ready to receive water. Fresh meat must be put in the cellar to protect it from freezing, or hung out in the open or in the forge to keep it as cold as possible without freezing. I would not want to live a life that was cut off from the seasons. *1965*

December 3 A quiet mild sunny day, cloudless, a light breeze upstream. A feel of spring in the air this morning, enough to stir one's insides; yet I cut firewood as usual. . . . A new moon, setting behind the hill before dark. Saw a great blue heron on the river. The remembrance of the city, of the traffic on the long avenue, the coldness, the inhumanity of the apartments; blocks of them, blocks of stones, the lights at night— *1956*

This whole day spent in trifles and small jobs, one after another; and even then I did not come to the end of all I had in mind. These chores are either necessary or desirable. The latter become critical after a period of time. It is good to set all these details to rights, even at the cost of the day; especially the long-standing ones. *1960*

A wintry day. . . . I began the winter season by building a fire in the forge and sharpening the big log saw. The fire heated the studio, prompting me to work up there the rest of the morning. The evening is dark and still, freezing. I think I keep up a cheerful spirit quite remarkably. I enjoy the dark bleak days, they are most homelike. A rift in the clouds, a piece of nice driftwood floating in, I rise into ecstasy. *1963*

There is something demonic about my woodcutting, like Moby Dick. I rise before day and in the moonlight even through clouds, I go out with saw and axe. . . . *1966*

December 4 I could have a power saw to cut our wood, and hire a tractor to haul things up from the river, but so many benefits and blessings attendant on hand work would be lost. *1956*

Printed woodblocks this afternoon, and played some [music]. In the attic yesterday I found a box containing small oil sketches done a long time ago—20 years and more. Set up 2 of them where they could be seen and I have enjoyed them. They are good. Perhaps I have been more successful than I thought. They are so simple and straightforward, artless; perhaps I will paint more. *1956*

We have read in Michael Levey's book, *A Concise History of Painting,* about the Italian painters of the Early Renaissance with great interest. To me, that is the best of it all. Those artists worked with innocence and freedom, their paintings were natural productions, with much in them that the artists were never aware of putting there. Modern art is thoroughly self-conscious and scientific. I feel that I work with a similar innocence, to some degree. Sometimes I wish I knew nothing at all about painting, could approach it with a fresh mind. One lives through the history of painting. It is ever taking a fresh start. As experience is gained, simplicity is lost—the old story. *1964*

December 5 Returned today from the north [a trip to Michigan], having been gone 3 weeks, minus one night. While I was gone I thought hardly at all of this place, and with no longing. Life centers at whatever place I happen to be living, and if it means walking the city pavements with Sambo, I arise eager to do it. Yet when I am here again, I know that my days were not complete when cut off from the earth. I would not last long in the city. Payne Hollow welcomes me. No person could be so kind, patient, understanding, loving. *1954*

While I am in the city, I am depressed, beaten down, I have gloomy thoughts about life and about myself, I think that there is something wrong with me, physically; as perhaps there is. . . . Here, I am strong and confident, able, composed, serene. No misfortune can touch me. . . . What I missed most of all, I think, was the open fire. How cheerless, how desperate, to be warmed by a fire you never see. I was never warm. *1954*

Gentle rains all this dark day. Now at nightfall there seems to be a wind from the NW, though the rain still falls. The goats were out in the woods for awhile, but came in during a heavier shower. They have had several sunny days of browsing and rest on the hillside. I like to see them filing down through the trees, nibbling here and there, each with his particular gait; or come upon them on some sunny bank among the leaves, their serenity putting to shame my business. How inane is most of my activity, cutting firewood for instance, when seen through their eyes. How complex and unbalanced my life is, compared with their simple existence. *1959*

All the world has said today, "What a beautiful day." The rain ceased in the night and the sun rose clear. . . . Up along the shore for a load of firewood. The atmosphere seemed not to exist, the river was an unruffled blue plane. I watched the lengthening shadows touch the eastern shore and spread until only the hilltops were in the ruddy sunlight. *1961*

I cannot write of nature with a poetic rapture or with a naturalistic keenness of observation. All I can hope for is to have something of what I feel come through in these trivial and commonplace facts. Perhaps I should try to express myself fully. In painting, however, I simply put down what I see and hope for the best. It is dangerous to interfere in this matter. *1961*

Yesterday the creek was running for the first time, clear water and a low sound. How much it adds, it is another form of life. *1964*

We get full value from cold weather—also from rain, snow, wind, sunny and cloudy skies, it all affects us more intensely, we seem closer to it. *1966*

December 6 I was up before daybreak this morning. The sky was cloudless, the air clear and calm. The stars bright, the moon being in the first quarter. By the light of the stars I tread well known paths, carrying buckets of sand up from the riverbank. The brilliant searchlight of a towboat flashing back and forth spoils the effect of starlight. After it is gone, I notice that one corner of Orion is down behind the western hill and the morning star has ascended in the east. A faint light can be seen there, my paths become somewhat lighter. The stars pale, and light floods the earth. What a blessing it is, given to us every day. *1956*

I see nature with a painter's eye. *1961*

We spent the afternoon in Classic Hall, Hanover College, talking with the few people who came to see us and my paintings. They were worth talking to, however, and I hope they found us so. It is encouragement and realized achievement to see that a picture takes hold of a stranger, not an artist or connoisseur, to the extent that he wants to own the picture, to have it be a part of his life. *1965*

December 7 From a mild day like this one, I look back on the recent cold weather as if it were on a higher level. The moon was late and I went down in its bright light, climbed the hill with axe and saw, cut wood. The eastern horizon lightened, the moon and stars paled. In the half darkness the coming light seemed a great unusual blessing. Now the keenness has gone from the air, the sky is soft and cloudy. *1955*

The dark heavy sky, portentous calm, heavy clouds building

up in the northwest, night extinguishing the feeble light of day. What gives a man courage to want to live, alone on this savage earth which is too much for him? A cold wind streams down from the northwest, the clouds already seem higher, they are breaking. It already seems possible that the stars will be seen tonight, and that the sun will rise clear. *1960*

December 8 I rejoice in the winter landscape, cut to essentials. Earth and sky are more closely joined. *1954*

Another clear morning. Orion is my clock. When its lowest star is down close to the western hilltop, it is time for me to get up. It was before the beginning of dawn when I went out this morning. An owl hooted far off, then suddenly one just across the hollow, giving a loud "who-o"; after an interval, another. The river was calm and smooth, the three stars of Orion's belt reflected in the water just over the johnboat. The simple masses of night's landscape. I went out along the path and began to saw firewood as the light of the coming day began to show in the east. *1961*

Monday AM I butchered, the sacrifice being Booster the big buck, a hard task because we were good friends. Yet the contract must be kept. He died nobly, without a sound, hardly any struggling, so different from the young bucks who leap at the rope's end like a hooked fish. *1964*

December 9 A sudden wind in the night. A cloudy, cold day, with snow flurries, round pellets of snow. Yet it did not freeze. Still a booming wind. I work outside in the wind and mud, happily tinkering about the cistern and foundation and wood pile. Wheeling sand and block up the hill. *1954*

We awoke this morning to 4 inches of snow, and more falling. This came from the east, the day became warmer and the snow, at first light and dry, became slushy in a drizzling rain. The evening dark and still, no rain, the ground still covered with snow. For me it was a long peaceful day, indoors, writing notes this morning, in the afternoon built a fire in the forge, cleaned up the place, filed my two coarse tree saws, a double satisfaction. *1961*

December 10 Everyone agrees that black locust when dry makes the best heating wood. Personally I think some kinds of oak equal it. *1955*

This is the best climate in the world. After two sunny quiet days, neither warm or cold—who would want perpetual summer?—now a gentle rain is falling as it grows dark after a quiet gray day. Think of snow, and starry nights like these last ones, and a fog frost such as the morning before this last one, when every twig is white. Who would not want some bad weather, even unpleasant days outside? *1959*

A cloudy day, though the night was starry and the early morning white with frost. At nightfall a mizzling rain of spring. Falling river left a mess of driftwood on the bar. I walk out on it for the first time after it has been under water as if treading a new earth, and I look into the driftwrack to see what treasures the river has left there. *1964*

December 11 Living beside a river which runs north and south, we see plainly the shifting winds. A south wind, against the current and with a longer reach, soon raises long, breaking swells and causes a steady uproar. The north wind sounds in the trees across the creek and its short choppy waves toss the johnboat, since they strike it broadside. *1956*

Who can explain the charm of bad weather, of crossing the river with rain in your face, of cutting wood on the wet hillside, the light rain pattering on the leaves? *1964*

The river and the hills are misty, our life seems closed in and circumscribed, and one is content. As the early darkness falls we make a light supper and are reminded of the wet outdoors only by the sound of rain on the roof. *1961*

In our living quarters, 3 fires burn—the fireplace, the cookstove and a movable oil heater near the windward door. It is quite comfortable and cozy. There is an exhilaration, a holiday spirit, about extremes of weather, especially these bright days, cold as they are. It is like the spirit aroused by the flooding river. *1962*

The sound of running water in the creek is our constant music. *1966*

I must mention the flock of large birds which went over southward in the bright morning sunlight of Dec. 3, Saturday. I was first attracted by their rattling, barking noise, loud and percussive. They flew in a wedge like Canada geese, but were definitely not, being lighter underneath. Size so near to Canada geese, I could not say they were larger or smaller. Several small flocks. Each one seemed bewildered by Payne Hollow across their course, for they circled and conversed about it before straightening out to continue on their way. *1966*

December 12 It may be considered a narrow limited life, but merely to do these simple acts, to enjoy these plain sensations over and over, are, we hope, enough to make one happy and contented. To arise in the frosty morning at the point of daybreak, climb the hill and cut wood, while the sky lightens above the soaring trees; to eat this wholesome, sweet food, to use my body, hands and mind at the endless work I have to do; to read by the firelight, to sleep warm and snug; all this shared and enjoyed by my loving partner—what manner of a man originated this idea of a happier life beyond death? *1955*

A mild quiet day, some pale sunshine in the morning, the afternoon cloudy. This is Ohio River winter. *1956*

I arose during the night to replenish the fires. The moon was striding across the clear sky, dimming the stars. It would have been sacrilege then to burn unholy fuel oil, but the wood cut from this hillside fed an altar flame. *1962*

Yesterday and today on a trip. . . . The comforting part is the return to the river. This evening it was very calm, the hills dark and severe, the smooth water dark with reflections from the hills and somber sky. . . . On such contacts as this with the city, living in a modern house on a city street, even for one night, I feel as if I had been subjected to an inimical force, and had suffered from it. I marvel that people can live balanced and serene lives in such an environment. Can they? From this viewpoint they seem strange, abnormal creatures, striving for the unattainable. Yet they are happy and would not change their way of living, certainly not for the mean and toilsome life that I lead here. *1963*

What church or shrine could be as holy as the river was this dark evening? This earth is a fit setting for a noble life, for one of peace and joy. *1963*

December 13 A fine winter day. Talk of the Mediterranean sky, it could not be more blue or clear than the sky I saw today, over a russet hill, through bare trees of gleaming silver. *1961*

The night was most clear, the brilliant moon past full was never dimmed, the morning star rose like a sun. *1962*

December 14 I am constantly ashamed of my weakness and meanness. I sometimes think that everyone is better than I am. I say, feel and do things that no one else would. I have not the poise and serenity one would expect from a person my age. *1960*

The other evening, when I stopped on the footbridge and looked down the stony creek bed, between the lines of trees, some tall pale sycamores, toward the river, with a glimpse of the blue hills beyond—I suddenly felt a great love for this place. It has become part of me. *1965*

December 15 Mild weather. Out in river yesterday afternoon and again today, cutting and picking up firewood along the rocky shore. . . . It is a definite pleasure to cut and handle the dead elm branches dried by the summer sun, the bark peeling off to expose the smooth hard surface. *1959*

A mild, sunny winter day. I was out at 5 o'clock, did the wooding for the day by moonlight. The hopes and uncertainties of the coming day, what will it bring? *1962*

December 16 Yesterday morning we heard the well-known, ominous sound of ice in the river, the moving floes grating against ice frozen along the shore, not a loud sound, but gentle, like rippled water; thus we knew the ice was not heavy. When daylight came we saw the river mostly covered with large sheets of new ice. I made a trial run with the outboard and found the ice could be broken through where it was not possible to find open water; so we made our trip as scheduled. *1958*

On some days the most precious part is in the early morning, that time after I get up before there is enough light to work outside. I build the fires and sit by the fireplace writing a few words by its light. Looking back on this hallowed time from the later hours of the day, it seems unreal, to belong more to night and dreams than to the waking day. *1960*

River rising again, it has carried away the snags on the bar before we had time to become acquainted with them. *1961*

December 17 A dark, drizzling morning, chill and dark. . . . Called on the McMahans. The buoyancy and cheerfulness, the faith of their life as it used to be seems to be fading, undermined by illness. It is depressing, on such a day as this, and I came home to my puttering. Man's life on this earth—who has courage to face it? Yet there are the trees, against the dark sky, black bare trees, springing from the earth to flower, swaying in the wind, the low hollow moan of the wind. Who could live without this grace? *1964*

December 19 Another still, thick day; a few splatters of rain. How gentle is the course of day from morning to night, there is little change from light to dark. We awake at daybreak, and watch the river emerge from the darkness, the trees become sharp and black against the lightening sky. Here there is no thought of time, no lights in surrounding houses, reminding the lay-abeds that some souls are up and doing, getting an early start on the day ahead. *1952*

I go up the hollow in the early twilight with my axe, cut a fallen sycamore branch in two and carry it in. In a few minutes, which are really devoted to [observing] the snowy valley, so opened by the snow, I get enough wood to burn half a day. The sweetness and peace of the snowy earth, transformed from that of yesterday, touches me deeply as ever. How it persists! What religious devotion could elevate and console as it does? It is simple and direct as if God spoke. Yet the words of a bible could not say what it does. *1954*

December 20 My allies are the rain, the peace of the dripping woods as I walk up the hill, and treasures beyond numbering. *1962*

The stars are wonderful, a grand view of the sky when I went down to the water's edge before daylight. *1963*

Christmas now is a manifestation of degeneracy. Like all religious observances, it has become entirely social. Even in this light it is no success. *1965*

December 21 While I cut wood in the short interval between sunset and dark, up the hollow, the sound of a hoot owl came from far off, a wooden sound like the beat of a savage drum, so in harmony with the winter sky and the fading light, and the sound of the axe. *1955*

Painting is unthought of in these cold days—no, not unthought of. *1963*

December 22 The longest night will be fully experienced this dark weather. It has rained gently this afternoon, so mild that winter cold is beyond thought, almost. I do keep it in the back of my mind, and will not be surprised by its blasts, which I will welcome. . . . We are enjoying our snug shelter on the hillside these dark wet days. I enjoy too the rainy sky and the sodden fields, the bare landscape. . . . The changing season reflected in a familiar landscape. Each month is different. *1952*

Much we do is required of us by urgent necessity. It must be done at once, often, yet this is not like having to do certain tasks by the clock, or meet daily obligations, the accomplishment or fulfillment of which produces no direct result. I must cut wood to keep warm, but when the wood is cut, there it is burning in the fireplace. Also, there is a positive choice, an eager willingness about the work I have to do, with rare exceptions. *1953*

In the darkness now I hear the river. *1962*

Fog and frost yesterday morning. When the tardy sun came out it revealed the frostwork on the trees above us, every branch and twig. *1964*

December 23 I rowed across to Lee's landing. . . . Payne Hollow exhibits new beauty when seen from the river now. This afternoon I wandered about, making some sketches, looking at birds. *1952*

Another mild day. Strong wind from south, and the river

was its roughest, the waves accented by the lowness of the sun. The morning perfectly clear and still. I was out before daybreak, beguiled by the starlight, which was enough to guide me wheeling firewood up from Payne's landing. *1957*

I was getting stone out of the creek, to be used in the foundation of the new wing on the studio. Stone is solid and heavy, and uncompromising. That is why I love it. One must work slowly with it and not expect fast progress. *1965*

December 24 Heard a song sparrow singing today, and many ducks on the river, their quacking in the fog a barnyard sound. Sometimes it is a definite pleasure to write a few words like that. It goes with cutting wood, taking a hot bath, or working well with tools. *1955*

Up the hill after dinner, for the last of the Christmas mail. As I mount the slope, my busyness falls from me, I am again conscious of that distant contemplative spirit, yet so near and real, that watches the writhings of men. *1962*

A fine walk through untrodden snow at sunset, especially through the cedars. The snowy landscape has new accents. *1963*

This evening is calm and bright, the moon half full, Venus in the west—what a Christmas star! And they do not notice it, shining from the clear sky over the snow, but go on mumbling old words of someone who saw a star long ago. *1963*

December 25 Yesterday we spent entirely on the hill, morning and dinner with Owen and Daisy, calls in the afternoon at the Watsons' and McMahans'. We stumbled down the hill in the darkness, carrying a load of gifts—a live hen and a jar of honey from Owen, a wild duck just shot by Wayne, and a piece of sausage from the Watsons, eggs and a piece of cake from McMahans. *1952*

Above all, I feel more than all concerns the imminency of death to each one of us. From this viewpoint what matters anything that we can do, or what happens to us? *1953*

On Christmas Eve the stars shone bright, and it was clear at sunrise, though part or most of the night was cloudy. I saw again the red tint of the sun on the upper half of the Indiana hills, the lower part in shadow. We saw no one today, but had a visitor yesterday. The two mallards he left with us were roasted for dinner today. . . . We observed Christmas with many of the usual trappings, unashamed and happy. I did some woodcutting. *1961*

Wind came around to N, after easy rain in the night. It has blown hard all day, and is still making a rough river, yet the air is calm around the house. How many people have not seen another person all this day? The day has been dark, unrelieved bleakness. One must depend upon himself. Yet think of all the consolation and good cheer that have been put into books and music. *1965*

December 26 If the goats understood my activities they would think me an inferior being—if they knew, for instance, that I killed and ate some of their number all the while showing friendly feelings to them, or if they realized how much time and strenuous toil I give to cutting wood which we must burn to keep us warm. *1959*

A trip to Madison, Milton, Hanover this PM, without accomplishing much. How strange it would be to live in those houses we entered, they are so closed in, so cluttered, so aimless, without character. Two of them had windows to the floor, and that was good, but one could hardly see through them for draperies and other hindrances. Yet people are good and friendly, and well-wishing, cheerful in appearance and brave. I have seen no one that I did not like. *1961*

December 27 Painting in the studio yesterday afternoon. Good. It brings everything into balance and harmony. *1964*

December 28 I need to be closer to the earth than I have been lately, to live more in the present moment, to keep up with the weather and season. Only thus can moral and mental and physical health be attained. *1953*

Probably no moon has furnished me with as much light as this one, in this clear weather. Now it is past full, and I can arise before daybreak and see my way about, sawing firewood. One feels alone on earth, no sounds, no lights, anywhere, unless a boat passes. In a light fog, as this morning, the isolation is even more strongly felt. It brings peace, contentment and a sure faith that all is well. *1958*

December 31 I have plodded through the day, chores to do after being gone yesterday. Water to pump, and considerable to-do getting equipment together and the engine running (at such times you wonder if it is worth it); then, with bad weather threatening, I worked at woodcutting. Now at twilight, the snow is falling, heavily, straight down. The ground and trees are already white. We are bathed and resting, the goats are fed and housed, I look forward to the darkness and night with peace and serenity. The far shore, the river itself, they are lost in the snow, all becomes white and gray. *1959*

January

January 1 The year opens, as the previous one closed, with fair, dry weather; the river clear and in low pool. *1956*

My chief concern at this present time is the fireplace and chimney which we are building in the new wing. It must be good, since it is the central feature of our living. I am sure it will answer our hopes. I can tell by the way I am working, by the pleasure I have in that and in the material. *1956*

As for creativity in art, my life is and has been unproductive. I feel stirrings within sometimes, and wonder how it will break forth. *1956*

A New Year's call today from 4 Bedford high school boys, fine chaps, full of eagerness and curiosity, sensitive and well-mannered, outspoken and friendly. *1957*

A gray day, yet in the early morning the western hills were briefly tipped with red-purple from the rising sun, at midday the clouds were broken and in the evening they were tinted with mother-of-pearl, such as Thoreau often describes. *1963*

On Monday we went to Madison, Milton, Hanover. In the latter place we called on two houses where friends live. One of them talked seriously and thoughtfully about our living here, and I tried to answer. Neither of us could express ourselves, because he had no idea of my outlook and I could not explain it. So we talked obliquely. They decide I have negative values, not accepting contemporary ways of action, that I am trying to hold to values and ideals of the past. Yet I see what no man has yet seen. I live in my visions, they live under a roof. I do not turn from society. There is no society, only people, and they are all good! *1964*

The river fell several inches last night. . . . This change of level has affected me deeply. I feel a great loss, irreparable. *1965*

An old person is praised for keeping up to date with the times, but I think he should be true to his generation. With his past experience and knowledge of old ways and ideas, he can never enter completely or understand the new. Instead of casting away his conceptions, his integrity, he should cling to them, and be an example to be cherished and revered by those of the present generation who care to look back. *1965*

In painting I feel sometimes that I have come to an end, and must make a new beginning. Again, it seems that all I have to do is continue in the same way. Yet what if I can produce nothing by the old methods? The lot of any sincere artist is hard, these days. A living art has been achieved in the past, and may never be again. *1965*

A soft steady rain began at nightfall yesterday, and continued all through this day. . . . Creek running strongly, a good sound not heard for some time. When I went down to feed the goats after daylight this morning, I found none of them. . . . They went up to the cliffs. . . . I went up there to see about them, and there they were, a fine sight as I looked up at them, the rock face towering above them and shelving out overhead. The goats were all in different positions, though close together, staring down at me and the dogs, motionless. Some were in niches of the rock, at different levels, like statues placed there. I spoke a few words to them, which they did not acknowledge at all, and then left them. *1966*

January 2 One lives on the frontier always, facing death, self-dependent in an unmapped wilderness. Yet we hope to live, expect to. *1956*

Instead of dashing through the day, completing one activity as quickly as possible so as to get at something else, it would be better to savor each part of the day as if this were your last day. Get as much out of the present moment as possible, from daybreak to bedtime. Even sleeping should be done well, even if one must wake up now and then to enjoy the night. When you eat, give each dish its full importance and extract its individual flavor. . . . Most everything we do deserves reverence, and a special setting. But one must live naturally, without pretense. *1961*

What do people have to base their life on, if it is not a love of nature? *1962*

Warmer today, with a south wind. Sunny all day, a colorful sunset, as so often this winter. Snow began to melt in the afternoon, and as I worked in the studio, I listened to the snow sloughing off the roof, landing on the snowy ground with a soft impact. Then drops and trickles of water began, at different rates of speed. At sunset and after, I do the last chores, watching the flaming and fading light. For me this is a requisite without which the day would be incomplete. *1964*

Rain in the night again, and a dark, showery morning, mild and springlike. The rain brightens the colors of the landscape, there are unexpected greens—of the box elder twigs, fresh grass in the meadow, the strong green of cedars. *1965*

I did some exciting painting this afternoon. Every picture is an experience, an adventure, not to be done by reason; previous experience cannot be depended upon. *1965*

January 3 All through the starry night the river was noisy with wind waves. The last of the moon rose just before daybreak, a false dawn. I was up then, out in the mild air, sawing a dead honey locust log (or blackthorn), the light increasing slowly as the day broke. The sun shone all day, the south wind roughing the river, now in pool. *1962*

After a break, however long, I begin painting again easily and naturally, and with added power; at least it seems so when I first begin. As always, a little productive work in this line lifts time and living to a new plane. I wonder how many painters have the satisfaction of expressing themselves, I mean, themselves, not just painting? *1962*

River rose sharply Sunday. . . . It is a real river again, current and drift, sound of broken water. *1966*

I am cast down by the remark often heard, "There hasn't been any winter yet." Have I been deceiving myself? What are these days, if not of winter? The ground is so frozen that the digging of parsnips required much hacking. The relation of most people to the weather, to the earth they live on, is loose and indirect. Winter must bludgeon them, the finer shades make no impression. They are so insulated from cold that they feel only the extreme temperatures. They are not outside long enough for the cold to penetrate. *1967*

I was up too early this morning, enticed outside by the quiet air and bright moonlight (though the moon was only half-full). I ground wheat and soy flour, then went out around the shoulder of the hill to cut wood. Felled two good-sized trees and cut them into sections I could handle. At length, light appeared in the eastern sky, colorless. The hooting of a horned owl. I came back to the house, started the fires. *1967*

January 4 Colder. The dry sharp air, after the moist warm days past, is a tonic. It is like a drink of cold water to a thirsty man. The sun shines, a rare sight this winter, but now it is dark, snow-like. The business of living is difficult enough, at times the obstacles seem nearly too much; then the knot is untied, and all goes smoothly. *1953*

I could write about nothing but myself. I sometimes entertain the idea of writing a book, a critical study of Thoreau, for instance, a book on aesthetics. Such are the tasks of a professional writer, which I am not. However, it seems that I should have a book in me: a member of a very small minority, what I have encountered in the world, what I have essayed, what I have experienced, thought, done. Everyone is an individual, of course. His inner life, truly and fully told, would be astonishing to any reader. *1953*

Man is riding high, now, particularly the young generation. They believe all is to be conquered by expanding the techniques now available. There is to be no limit, no restraint. Of course they scoff at the contrary person who still uses an axe, saw and oars. They should encourage him as a rare specimen, furnish him tools and opportunity to use them. *1964*

For dinner today we roasted a piece of goat back, first wrapping it carefully in aluminum foil, then putting it in hot coals for two hours. It was delicious, being tender, moist, with a roasted flavor. We consider it the best meat we have cooked. *1963*

Some painting in the afternoon, and we played our new

music. Schubert sonatas for violin and piano op.137 and Schumann, op.121. *1965*

Today I reached the legal age of retirement [65], but this like other days has been unaffected by the calendar. I still feel my best work is ahead. *1965*

January 5 I was out on the hillside sawing a log by moonlight. A large part of the time I am merely vegetable, simply enjoying this earth on which I live; the sunlight, winds, smells, sights and sounds. Yet as a man I am blessed with so much more than any other animal, because my greatest pleasure is supra-sensual; also, I have memories and reflections. May I be pardoned if this is presuming too much. *1961*

I pulled across the river this morning to get 4 sacks of ear corn for the goats. The water was smooth, the sky gray, so that water and sky were so much alike that I might have been rowing in the sky. The familiar often-studied reflections of the land were undisturbed, and my passage could be noted only by a bit of drift, or by the shifting of the tree line as it opened or closed the distant shore. *1963*

The goats came into the stable this evening, their breaths smelling of onions. They gather the first spring greens. *1965*

Never leaving this hollow and this particular shore, I am limited in my subjects for painting, yet one could paint a lifetime from just one viewpoint. *1965*

Another rainy day, after two fine ones. There was a sweetness about this mild dark morning that suggested spring—and a dove sang. *1966*

January 6 The danger is to see and hear with the intellect instead of the senses, or rather with the intellect alone, instead of the intellect through the senses. Nothing is more perishable than our relation with the earth. It must be constantly renewed. Come in a house, think of something else, become absorbed in some work—it is gone. This communion is only possible when the mind is free. The body may be doing whatever it wants to do. *1963*

No woodcutting, a little painting, cleaned the stable partly, dug some parsnips, bailed the johnboat, went over stuff in the cellar, played some music at the end, until after sunset when the light fails. We both look forward to this time with pleasure and usually are not disappointed. *1964*

Painting in the afternoon. . . . The requirement is continuity, day after day. Then, even when not painting, it is on your mind, you see pictures. It is possible that new fields are opening to me, new freedom, a new aim, which might be the synthesis of abstract and representational painting. Yet always each picture will be an entity, not necessarily related to what was done before. *1965*

January 7 I use some discipline in the conduct of a day, allowing myself but little relaxation or slackness, always trying to get as much done as possible and to have some of it worthwhile and unique. *1961*

A rough wind, driving straight down the river, unbroken cloudy sky. At the day's beginning the clouds seemed to lie on the earth. *1966*

The moon gives light in the evening and morning, thus extending the working day. *1966*

January 8 Such a quiet warm day, we went to town, thinking of swift water and windy days to come. . . . It was dark when we reached our landing today, cloudy with rain perhaps imminent. We worked fast unloading and loading. We rowed across the dark river, rough in the south wind, toward the dark shore. Leaving here is hard and inconvenient at times, but on each return we experience a joy at being here; a feeling which we forget when we go among other people. *1954*

I have given my best to this fireplace, not hurrying, making no compromises. *1956*

I was out on the hillside, slippery with the light snow, cutting wood at sunset—sunset over the snow, the sound of an axe in the woods. *1962*

The danger is that one accepts his emotions, takes them for granted. They become familiar to him, lose their vitality. We must be honest here, and not say we love where we feel no love. It is not a matter of reason or determination. *1962*

It will be a dark rough night, and a cold windy day tomorrow. Now, at the height of winter, and of our resistance, we do not mind how cold and windy it is. *1964*

January 9 What would I do with a whole day, or a series of them, all to be devoted to painting, with no interruptions? For me, these short periods between other work is better—all good painting that I do is done in a flash. Planning and niggling accomplish nothing. You must get up steam. When the pressure is high enough, the engine starts to run. *1961*

I dipped water out of the creek, some of it in the darkness of early morning. When I went down this evening for more, the creek was dry. I went to the spring, which is running well. River has been rising slowly, the bar is nearly covered, water roily. Shad for dinner. It is food to be especially thankful for, so bountiful coming in this season of dearth, so easy to take—and delicious, withal. *1964*

January 10 A cloudy day, with no glimpse of the sun; a north wind, and at evening a drizzling rain. This is the first bad weather of the year, and it is good. *1956*

I am conscious of the longer days. I seem to have a keen sense of time, in a certain way, knowing just when the light should come and go. Now there is definitely more daylight, and the dawn comes sooner. *1956*

January 11 The past three days have been real winter, the most wonderful days of the winter, perhaps. The sky is most clear, the stars at their brightest, the moon nearly a quarter full this evening. The mornings are best. This morning as I cut wood on the south sloping hillside, the familiar world was transformed, a new sky, a new air, good to breathe. The air was filled with frost crystals which could be seen plainly as they moved across the path of the sun. They reflected the sunlight like rippled water. Intricate frost work on the creek where the water still runs. The little pool under the footbridge is frozen over, the thin ice covered by an amazing pattern of frost flowers. Some hilltops had frosty trees, and as I looked toward the sun as it rose over the hill south of us, I saw it shining through trees of lacy white along the crest of the hill which was all dark underneath. *1962*

This morning the temperature was 4 degrees. . . . I feed the fires all the wood they will take, and last night was up three times to refuel. I enjoy it all, even the bedtime trip to the [goat] stable, with a bottle of hot milk and a bucket of water. *1962*

Some woodcutting and writing in the morning, most of the afternoon given to painting, which is very exciting just now. It is strange how it goes along, rather doesn't go, regardless of the effort. Then suddenly it clicks, you do things you have dreamed of for a long time. *1965*

Surprised by some visitors, 5 of them, who walked down the hill late in the afternoon. Local people. The farm people are understanding, their comments are thoughtful and sincere. *1965*

January 12 Wind all night under the flaming stars. *1954*

Yesterday we drove to Richmond, Indiana to visit the Staeblers. . . . It becomes more and more strange and uncomfortable to live in conventional houses, though I do it easily for a short time. They are so shut in, even the windows seem not to look out of doors; and the people who live in them are little, or not at all, concerned with the earth on which they live. Outside is just a change of temperature, a region to be passed through as quickly as possible to get to another airless cave. At night I am bothered by the eternal light and by the unabating heat and dryness; yet I love the people who live there, admire and respect them. *1961*

January 13 I saw a turtle (terrapin) rambling in the woods today. *1958*

I have always kept shy of specialization and distrusted this rigid and extreme division of labor, but perhaps a man cannot do one task well unless he does give his whole time and energy to it. With all the varied work he must do, who would provide for himself, and all the demands on his time, how can he do anything really well? I must think this over. If a man could simplify his life until his wants were so few that he could provide for them by only little expenditure of time and attention, he might then give the best part of himself to his specialty. Certainly, no one should be so one-sided as to give all of himself to one pursuit. And perhaps a man's true work is done quickly, a sudden flowering. *1962*

Yesterday to Milton, Madison, Hanover. My chance meetings with people are seldom satisfactory. I feel afterwards that I have been awkward and obtuse, inconsiderate. *1965*

January 14 I save time and steps by carrying water to the goats from the inside tap, but I prefer to carry it from the creek, a long haul sometimes. This evening I found a clear pool after passing some ice from under which the water had all drained. As I dipped into the pool I saw the golden half moon reflected there, and was glad I came. *1962*

Our guest left Sun. PM having taken all our time, our lives and thoughts while he was here. *1963*

This was one of the rare mornings of the year, a clear sunrise over the snowy earth, fog on the river, frost crystals in the air, floating through the path of the sun's light. When the fog cleared the riverbank trees were all made of crystal, as were the woods on our hill. *1964*

January 15 What did I do this rainy morning? I was up quite a while before daylight and first cleaned the furnace flue, since the fire in the furnace was out. Then I changed tubs in the outhouse. As it was still dark, I lit a lamp, wrote a little until light enough to feed and milk the goats. After breakfast I made a fire in the shop, cracked some walnuts, sharpened my axe on the grindstone, scraped two goat hides in the process of tanning, ripped some boards into strips to use in framing. Before dinner I dipped up shad, cleaned and cooked them. . . . No woodcutting today. *1961*

The days are rounded out smoothly as the passage of the sun. It is morning, and then it is evening, and what has been done? Perhaps nothing is required, only a cheerful, hopeful spirit, confident of the unknown future. *1964*

January 16 We went to Madison on several errands. . . . We arrived at the shore just before sundown and our hill was glowing with warm color, the slash of Payne Hollow revealed by dark blue shadows from the low quartering light of the setting sun. Soon the shadows began to climb the slope and the whole range became dark. *1961*

What force is it that drives me to work, to try to make all the time in the day count for something? . . . This morning I returned to woodcutting with satisfaction. What would I do without this daily occupation? I would not care to spend the entire day in my studio. Music, reading, even writing can be indulged in only late in the day, when the outside work and painting are done. *1961*

Painting is exciting business. The possibilities are without limit, and the bleak unproductive times passed through make the good days seem even richer. *1961*

The times of the day are so different one to another that I seem a different person in each. Will the I that writes this by lamplight in the chill dark hour at daybreak, feeling the uncertainty of the long day before me, be the same person that puts down a few words in the twilight after the day has closed and shown itself to be like the preceding days after all? *1961*

The snow is beautiful under the full moon. . . . Every bit of color, a faded goldenrod or a withered leaf, has its effect now. *1965*

This morning and yesterday or day before, this hillside was alive with robins, thousands of them, chattering softly among themselves, as they fed on the dry berries of the hackberry trees. Heard the wings of a dove as I walked up the hill. *1965*

Men try for too much, they are presumptuous. Who could step out of the path laid for him on this earth by past generations? A man is nearly blind, only dimly perceptive; yet he pretends to choose and select, to order his life by his intellect. The wisest man is a duffer. *1965*

This is winter, after all. A cold penetrating wind from NE, indirectly felt here. When we crossed back across the river last night it was blowing hard out there. Faint, chill stars overhead, cold, cheerless lights along the road, not friendly houselights. *1966*

January 17 This was a cold morning, close down to zero. With no wind and a bright sun, it is pleasant to be outside. I cut some of the wood along the path, small convenient trees reserved for snowy weather. Made a sketch from the window of the goat shed. . . . It is most pleasant to look out on the snowy landscape. A richness has been added. *1965*

January 18 These have been sunny, quiet, winter days; indigenous, native weather, without incursions from north or south. *1961*

I cut a sound ash tree 12 to 14 inches in diameter. Cutting such a tree is a rite, rarely indulged in, and fully appreciated and valued. *1961*

I arise in the darkness. When I first go out, there seems to be light enough for work in the woods, but after a fire is lighted, the darkness is more intense, and I must light the lantern. The blessed sound of running water. It is more distant in the darkness, morning and evening. There are people who are awakened by the stale sound of radio. What can their lives amount to? *1962*

Yesterday to Louisville, making an early start on the frosty morning, with 20 of my paintings, 17 of which we hung in the Lincoln First National Bank in the Mall Branch, one of a series of shows run by the Guild Gallery. The space, walls and lighting were good, the severe interior offered no distractions and many people will see the pictures. There is a coldness and antagonism about the bank, but the paintings hold their own, I think. The comments of regular patrons of the bank, as they came in and saw a new exhibit, were revealing. "Hot dog, something I can understand at last," was the strongest and most spontaneous but others were of the same nature, if more subdued. I still believe that art is for the people. It need not cater to them. *1963*

A spectacle yesterday morning was the rare one of frost crystals shimmering as they moved across the path of the sun. *1965*

January 19 [After two weeks away:] Today we came back to Payne Hollow, back home. Here I become alive again, and dormant sensations and faculties begin to function. I come out of doors, too, as definitely as if I had left a closed room. I feel an inward joy. All that I had dreamed was true, is true. The earth is as fair, more fair, than I had known or imagined. *1953*

This was a warm day, still and misty, a faint sunlight filtering through. We drove over the hills and down along the river, watching the well-known features of the winter landscape. The recession of trees into the blue distance, the faintly green hillsides, many shades of tawny and russet, the sharp white sycamores, the slanting lines of the hilly country. After passing Carrollton and branching off to follow the river down, we become eager to reach the end of our journey. . . . Milton, and we are almost there. . . . We turn off the highway. Already the country is closer, more real. The known farmsteads pass by, the road turns and we leave it for the gravel: it is like stepping down from the pavement onto the cool earth. *1953*

Our friend says, "You have the right idea, I would like to live like you do. Away from the rush and hurry, no gadgets, a simple life, etc." All the while his wife is noncommittal, but with her own ideas how life should be lived. I believe the man's dissatisfaction with the accepted way of life is sincere, and he would like to make a change for the better, but what that better would be, he is not sure. The human race subconsciously mistrusts the artificial. It feels that it is getting too far away from the natural way. Yet this man is committed to the course from which mankind cannot turn back. We are exceptions to a degree. Only in exceptional cases would it be practical or desirable to live as we do. Aesthetic reasons are the stronger. *1961*

January 20 I still have dreams of an earthly life on a higher level, more honest, more simple, more remote, on the very fringe of society, from which I will accept only the barest necessities. *1963*

Sometimes I awake in the morning with a surge of joy, and eagerness for activity on all fronts, a firm faith that the best is yet to be. *1964*

January 21 I go down to bail out the johnboat, and the view up the river has something of grandeur. The mist sets off the hills to their different distances, and the opening between the two points is like a gateway to a land far away. Plowhandle Point rises mountainlike. This view is one of our greatest assets here. It has classic dignity. Yet I have never painted it at all satisfactorily. *1962*

Yesterday late in the afternoon I went up for the mail; returning, the landscape seemed the essence of winter. The light snow made a fine showing among the cedars and rocks, the narrow white road leading down into the dark valley. The low sun was in a pale golden haze, with slate colored clouds in layers. Against this sky the bare tips of trees— *1962*

I butchered a goat, Richwood, this morning. . . . People say, How can you do it, a friendly goat like Richwood who has been a pet? Perhaps it is a kind service to end anyone's life. Who in this world is of any use, except to his family, and even that is not so, it turns out in many cases. Those who are doing significant, irreplaceable work are very few. *1963*

Quite a heavy fog this morning, and frosted trees, every one from river to hilltop. When I was sawing wood on the ridge the sun came out brightly there, the whitened trees rising into the blue sky, while down in the hollow all was frost, fog and snow. *1965*

January 22 Cleared this afternoon but quite a cold day, especially on the hill, where the east wind blew. Quiet down here, but we hear the incessant sound of wind in the trees atop the south hill.

> The burning of fire, now the blaze increases
> with the fresh wood; now it diminishes
> as the wood is consumed; this is the time
> of greatest heat; then the air chills and
> we pile on more wood. It is the rhythm
> of all things, the rise and fall of the river,
> the pulse of life itself. *1954*

The creek is running out strong after successive showers last night and today. It is a good sound in the quiet valley. River rising a little. . . . I pick firewood out of the wet drift, as in shantyboat days, and it burns well. *1957*

Light snow during the night. I step out—and spoil its perfect cleanness. Such is man's life on this earth. *1961*

I dreamed of rising water and the johnboat tied up out of sight. After that I could not sleep until I went to the river bank to see how it was. The rain had slackened temporarily and enough moonlight filtered through the clouds to light my way. The boat was all right, but I bailed it out and tied it higher up the bank. Now I could sleep. *1962*

The snow transforms the earth, and affects our living in every detail, and our thoughts. I cut wood for an hour or two this morning, rejoicing in the snowfall and the new landscape—new, yet old effects seen how many times, and how long ago? This evening, indoors is more cozy than ever, with all the chores done, the goats in the stable and satisfied, fires burning brightly and enough wood at hand. Mellow lights to write and read by. A towboat passes downstream, sweeps the house and snowy hillside with its searchlight, toots a signal for us. Food is good, and sleep is good. Then I will wake in the darkness of early morning, eager to go about my cold and snowy work. *1966*

January 23 Nearly every evening we play some music, piano with violin or viola, using the Aladdin lamp which is very satisfactory. These days we seldom take time during the day for playing, so the cello is neglected. We read together, after dinner, usually French or German, both looking at the book and reading by turns. I read a little after breakfast, and in the evening. When all the work is done for the day and music is over, we relax and read by the fire—one reading while the other is busy at some hand work, until one or both get sleepy, which is usually in a short time. Just now we are reading after breakfast, D.C. Peattie's book on trees—after dinner, *Naufrage Volontair*—evenings, Sophocles' *Ajax*, Henry James' *Bostonians,* a review of modern art, *The Silent World,* about free diving, and others. *1962*

Two degrees at sundown. . . . I have been very busy. Cut down a tree this morning, to be out and enjoy the snowstorm which was raging then, almost a blizzard. A driving mist concealed the river, and the shores across could hardly be seen through the mist and snow. I take emergency measures in the house and stable, stuffing up cracks, etc. There is the exhilaration of extreme weather, a holiday spirit, the joyful snow, the winter air. *1963*

In the afternoon I made a beginning in the studio, but was interrupted by the arrival of 4 Hanover students, to whom my afternoon was of no concern. *1965*

January 24 I cut saplings in the blackberry patch near the barn, where our best and most abundant berries came from last June. It is a satisfaction to work in the winter fields for next summer's benefit; to know that you will be here again to reap the good harvests. *1953*

Colder today, a stiff west wind which filters through the house. . . . An agreeable afternoon inside, puttering, playing [music], reading, looking out of the windows. From what does worthwhile writing spring? Knowledge, experience, craftsmanship? Perhaps anyone who could talk, if he had something important to tell, could write it down; perhaps he could write poetry of a high order if he were inspired to. The skill of words can go only so far. *1953*

River very rough this morning. It is of a strange color—an opaque gray, not muddy, like dirty melted snow. Perhaps this being the first rise in half a year it has washed the earth of a layer of dust and soot, as does the first rain on a roof. *1954*

To Madison. Hard pull across in strong wind from NW. A cold day. The dogs are always at the landing to welcome us home, in any weather, any time of day or night. *1961*

January 25 Sunday. We find it profitable to observe Sunday; not in absolute inaction, or complete laziness, but enough relaxation, extra reading, resting, and non-productive activity such as taking a walk. This allows us to run down, to become altogether—no, not quite that—at rest. *1953*

While I was cutting wood this evening, a tough piece of dry slippery elm, with a saw that could take a sharpening, working in the cold, raw wind at a task never finished, I asked myself just why I got our fuel thus, when others did so by much easier methods. I think the real reason why I object to imported fuel and mechanical devices is that they get between me and nature. They spoil my close relation to the earth, either by their mere presence, by their noise, smell or connotation. I would live as much out-of-doors as a bird, if I could. *1957*

The snow brings out the structure of the hills, the crests, slopes and rocky ledges. The trees are seen as a mere fringe or feathery growth against the smooth, solid hill. *1961*

I paint a little in the afternoon, enough to give a different spirit to the day. *1961*

The snow is clean and dry, the earth clean and hard. This is good winter. *1961*

I have made several attempts to begin the writing of a book which might have been called "Payne Hollow," but so far have not found the key. Perhaps the audience and the publisher have been watching me, demanding that I write something entertaining. I should write as I paint, with no thought that anyone will ever see the picture. *1963*

January 26 We imagine how our end will be, how death will come, but perhaps it will be like the end of a journey, which we think about on the way until we can almost see the path or road to the very end, but before arriving there, the road turns and changes, perhaps going over a hill or crossing a bridge we had never thought of, and often the way is much farther than we had imagined. *1962*

A gray sky, a white earth—between these are many subdued colors, shades of gray, almost black. The effects of the landscape are entirely strange after the snowless time, yet the effects of snow are just as familiar and known to me—the tawny grass, hardly noticed among the browns and russets, rises above the snow in a glowing cover, the blue cast on the distant woods, the warm cedars, the stark shape of bare trees. *1963*

The *chok chok* of an axe on a winter evening, the sun having set over the snowy earth, the new moon beginning to shine. *1966*

Man has evolved into this social, technological, intellectual animal, but perhaps another development is possible, in another direction. He need not modify and subdue the earth, his home, nor forget that he is part of the natural system. I hear a cardinal sing. *1966*

January 27 The moon set shortly before dawn, an ill-shaped copper mass to the north of west. The sky was full of stars, just beginning to pale. I was up in the near darkness, busy at what could be done without more light. As the radiance in the east increased I could do more. Light seemed a blessing. We take it so thoughtlessly. Soon my actions become complicated; I measured and calculated. It was day. *1953*

The winter rain falls heavier
as if waiting for the darkness.
Outside is chill and wet;
the rain makes a soft noise on the roof,
its sound ebbs and swells like music.
Within our wooden walls is peace and contentment.
The dogs sleep, the fire flickers and cheeps.
I think of the creek—is it running out?
No, the rain is too gentle and wayward for that;
the little johnboat I have tied in the creek mouth
is safe. It lies motionless where the muddy river
is met by the clean water from the spring in the hills. *1953*

I walk up the hill for mail, always a pleasant, inspiriting trip. *1954*

I love my tools, they are part of me, and if they are not sharp and well adjusted, it is as if I myself were out of sorts. *1961*

In the evening I give over the struggles of the day and withdraw inside. Wood for the night is in the cellar and I use the inside passage to feed the fire. Doors are battened, the cracks around the woodbox stuffed with strips of newspaper. Goats are tended and left in the warm stable. Dogs in with us. After being out in the cold so much during the day on this steep, windy hillside, I am astonished that on this site, by our own efforts, we can enjoy much comfort and security. *1961*

January 28 I found much satisfaction in hauling the rest of the red oak tree up the steep bank to wheelbarrow level by means of a block and tackle. *1963*

These days we see the noble aspects of winter, frostwork on the trees, especially along the river one morning when a fog came up after daylight. *1966*

January 29 8 degrees this morning, fair with fog over the river and ice. . . . A south wind and waxing moon. Why does a rising temperature give a feeling of security and peace? *1961*

A bright, clear morning, temp. zero. . . . Much open water in the other half of the river, where the ice is slowly moving. Long wet streaks on this side, but the ice holds. . . . It is arctic scenery, to stand out there and look over the expanse of white ice which stretches to the familiar shores. *1963*

I continued to work in the studio, building a hot, quick fire, which soon made itself felt. When the place cools off again, it is time to quit. Pleasant to go inside where it seems really warm, take off my outdoor clothes, and play some music. Then the evening chores—goats, johnboat, fires and whatever. Supper by candlelight before the fire, which after burning all day and getting the stones warm, puts out the heat. It would be nice to keep relaxed after supper, but there is another spell of action, the dishes to wash, goats to water, etc. Then until bedtime we can sit by the fire and read, not even going out for more wood, for I get enough in. *1965*

January 30 A clear night, full moon on the snow. All the illumination seems wasted on mankind. Even we make little use of it, except that it lights our way after dark—to the cellar, goat stable and about the room. *1961*

Yesterday I butchered the young buck, Flip, and though he was somewhat of a nuisance, the operation was not easy. Always I feel inferior to the animals I butcher. They rise above, I fall below. Yet I go through with it, hacking away with bloody hands, skinning the handsome head, whose unclosed eyes have a classic grace and serenity. *1962*

January 31 A cardinal, female, sung its spring song early this morning close to the house. *1961*

A surprisingly cold morning, about 8 degrees here. A brilliant day. After cutting down an elm tree, I set to work on the floor and kept at it until late in the afternoon. Then a little more woodcutting and chores. I find even a few hours on indoor work, especially with artificial, synthetic material like floor filler and varnish, to be depressing and unhealthy. I go out of doors and my spirits rise, I look into the blue sky, listen to the river noisy with wind and current, and feel sure that nothing in the future could be evil, unless it were too much varnish. *1962*

I am enjoying the constant snowy landscape. *1963*

February

February 1 We have descended from the heights of winter. *1955*

We have been reading a book on Chinese art by Michael Sullivan, an excellent book. . . . "Only by truthfully reproducing the visible forms of nature can the artist hope to express, through them, their deeper significance. . . ." Chinese painting has meant much to me. I remember the enthusiasm with which I read Lawrence Binyon's *Painting in the Far East,* in 1920. I don't know how it has influenced me, but perhaps I am something of a Zen Buddhist in painting. More and more I depend on those sudden flashes, often coming after a long period of reworking a picture with disheartening results. Then all at once, after almost destroying it, the picture clicks and I paint the whole thing very quickly, with the sureness of a Chinese master. My painting might be more formal than I realize, too, eclectic, using a few subjects over and over. But on the whole, there is something so strange and foreign in Chinese art that I am not at home there. It is almost repelling. *1964*

I butchered a goat this morning, a yearling buck. . . . As I was doing that laborious, messy job, out in the wind and snow and cold, I thought of indoor fires, books and music; looking up the snowy hillside, among the bare trees, I was conscious of a grace and tenderness, a beauty far above all art. I kept at the work in the afternoon. *1965*

Snow began to fall in the night—bare spots of ground were just whitened when I looked out. . . . This is one of the sights, one of the experiences I live for. *1966*

Winter takes over. The world's schedules are disrupted. *1966*

February 2 The bright moon lights the path
through the gray woods
From the unlit depths of the hollow
comes the soft sound of broken water
A faint brightness
or is it a low cloud
within the eastern sky
The earth is hushed 1953

A certain amount of courage is required to arise in the dark and cold every morning through the winter, to start the fires, have a look at the weather, go to the stable to feed and milk the goats, often with a lantern, which wakes them up. Each morning, however, I am eager to begin the day, and go about the same routine with zest. It is ever exciting to go out of doors, there is something that never becomes familiar or commonplace or routine. *1962*

February 3 Another fair day, that is, fair for winter. Morning cloudy, a hazy sun afternoon, and at night, bright stars. No wind, a perfect day for drifting. One could drift far this winter—no ice, yet, no flood, yet, little cold weather and wind. *1953*

We watched through our window a Carolina wren, who could not see us, apparently, it came so close. *1953*

A mild sunny day, the river smooth as the sky. Winter suddenly withdraws, leaving the landscape unchanged. It doesn't look right in the warm sun, without a sign of spring. . . . One relaxes at once in the warm air, the cold weather urge slackens, the routine of fires and wood cutting is broken. *1962*

The sign, "Paintings are not sold," was so confusing that I tacked a board over it. Then on an impulse I wrote another sign on the board, "No paintings for sale." That should be definite enough for everyone, except perhaps for a buyer who really wants a picture. Now I can paint without considering the possibility of selling. Not until now did I realize that there was even a slight pressure. *1964*

February 4 I cut a white oak for firewood. What hard and heavy wood! Picture frames again in afternoon, finishing two. I can make them quickly, with a simple and sturdy construction, using different woods from my stock—weathered barn boards or driftwood, black walnut, cherry, cedar, and some light-colored soft woods. A good frame enhances a picture right away. If it doesn't, no amount of tinkering will make a good frame of it. *1961*

Yesterday was cold, about 12 degrees in the morning, with light winds from N. We planned to go to Louisville to hear a quartet, if possible. The shore ice was still solid, the river was covered with large floating sheets of new-formed ice. Late in the morning I slid, pushed and pulled the johnboat over the ice to the end of the bar, being lucky in driving an iron bar through a crack in the ice into the stony bottom, a good anchor for the blocks, without which I could not have moved the boat over the last hummock of loose ice. Then it was possible to slide it out onto thin ice, which I cut away and rowed upstream in a streak of open water, until the narrow band of ice along the shore above Payne's landing was reached. Here I pulled the boat out onto the ice until we were ready to embark. An open space came by, but we missed it. When we started, the sheet of floating ice was unbroken, sometimes scraping the shore ice, sometimes leaving a channel wide enough for us to row upstream. Once we went out into some open water, but soon came to ice we could not break through. We rowed up as far as Moreland's Creek before reaching the end of the ice. Then we rowed across. *1963*

We crossed over today, after sliding the johnboat more than its length to get it in the water. Shore ice to break through. . . . Never saw a finer view of Payne Hollow than that from Lee's landing today as the sun was setting. The Kentucky shore was sharply lighted by its level rays, the deep shadow and tree masses in the hollow contrasting with the sunlit slopes where the separate trees had little effect, although the vertical lines of the trunks and the slanting lines of the thin shadows in the snow were evident. All the details were sharp and clear, the harmonies elemental. *1965*

February 5 This might be the best time of the year, for me. The fall work is done, the spring activity has not yet been started. Busy as I am every day, there is spaciousness to the days. I paint and play a little music by myself, experimenting and feeling for new ways. The days go by smoothly as the rotation of light and dark. Each morning I rise just as light begins to show, and each day holds great promise. *1958*

Today we come back to homely duties after yesterday's extravagance—the "reception" at Hanover College, opening the art show. It is strange to be the center of attraction; I feel like an impostor. I am uneasy, as if indecently exposed, when I see people looking at my paintings. Yet they were all friendly people, who meant well. I heard no intelligent or penetrating remark. *1968*

February 6 This morning we saw the sunrise of a new season. A bright clear sun when it first came over the ridge, the far hills showed a ruddy brightness while the river trees were in deep shadow. The day became cloudy, however, with some traces of snow. It is aimless weather, rather uninteresting when one thinks of Vermont or New Mexico, but still the earth and sky, clouds and misty hills, the rich landscape, tawny and purple, are of an unattainable beauty. *1954*

This was a rough day, with a strong cold wind from the NW, yet it was a brave sun which shone through the openings in the great white clouds, ragged and moving fast. Early in the morning the clouds were heavy, causing a violent snow squall, after which the clouds seemed to explode and scatter. It was quiet and warm on the south slope where I cut wood most of the morning. *1962*

My woodcutting is interrupted, and also my painting was yesterday, by the arrival of Hanover students walking down the hill. I seem to have no defense. They have a free afternoon and spend it by an excursion here, not realizing, I suppose, that they take up my afternoon. The only consolation is the possibility of their absorbing something from the visit that will stay with them. *1964*

Painting seems far away, but perhaps the pressure will build up and I will start again. The days seem pointless. *1968*

February 7 Early in the morning, a strange sound in the darkness from the river; it might be wind and waves, but no wind stirred. It was ice—heavy, broken pieces, from bank to bank, flowing on a swift current. By evening the ice was almost gone. *1963*

Snow flurries through the day; one of them transformed the landscape almost in an instant. The wet snow clung to everything and when I walked eastward along the path, all was white, every grass and twig. *1964*

Warmer yesterday and today, the snow melts away, bare ground appears on the hillside facing south. Considerable broken ice in the river today, but it thinned out. No wind, no sun today. After an effort I freed the johnboat from its icy bed and got most of the ice out of it. Feel better now. *1966*

The human race is caught in a trap. It is every man for himself. The only way out is to find a way back to a natural life, whatever the sacrifice. This is not for everyone. *1968*

February 8 We returned home [from a trip to town] midafternoon. After the fires were started and all stowed away, I went out on the hillside to cut some wood. It may be cold and bleak in town, but there among the trees above the creek, it is cheerful and I am warm. *1963*

February 9 Water running in all the creeks, cascading down the hill at the falls. *1965*

River rising sharply. A strong gusty wind tonight. A shantyboater would look to his moorings. *1966*

Wind came from NW today, slowly increasing in strength. It still blows into the night and great white clouds sail across the starry sky. *1968*

A fire in the studio this afternoon and some painting—repainting a small picture from week before last. I realize more and more that painting is not a reasoned, intellectual process. Means and method must be part of yourself, not requiring conscious thought and direction. *1968*

February 10 A warm sunny day, a day of spring. The earth and all its inhabitants relax. *1954*

We drove to Fort Thomas, returned. . . . The golden landscape, the high country between Rising Sun and Vevay, gashed by blue valleys, a flock of canvasback ducks on the river. *1954*

Who can say when spring begins? In the cornfield we found the tiny white flowers of the chickweed. *1957*

I see the goats, chewing their cuds and looking wise as philosophers. No doubt they are wiser than I. Do they feel the same joy in the blue sky and in the wind on the river? *1962*

It is as exciting as ever to have a rising river to watch. *1966*

February 11 An absence of even three days makes a decided break in our living here, it is somewhat strange at first. Town is so unlike. I feel a lifting of spirit each time I return here, an unspeakable welcome. *1953*

From a good painting emanates a glowing grace. It almost speaks. This is rare. Most painting is empty, dead, the paint itself sickening. When they wallow in the quaking bog of nonrepresentative painting, professional and amateur become so muddy that you can't tell which is which. This is an achievement the occasional painter cannot attain—to paint a picture so real that one can almost enter into it bodily. It might be that the forms are so pared down and simplified that they seem casual, but such simplification is the essence of much skill and experience. *1953*

What is the supreme achievement of the human mind? It is faith, a joyful, unquestioning belief that above the materials and mechanics of this earth is an unknown, unknowable, mysterious spirit which confounds all the probing of science. The path of science is a widening spiral, ever departing from the core of life. Faith is as certain and sure as the light and warmth of the sun. *1953*

I bought a new axe yesterday. . . . Some of the products of this machine age are beautiful, this axe is one of them. . . . I notice the length and slimness of the blade. *1953*

A large flock of robins in the hollow and about the house today, singing a little and chirping. I believe they passed on. I noticed for the first time the swelling and reddening of the soft maple buds in trees along the creek. This is a certain sign of spring; suddenly it is to be seen; just when does it begin? *1953*

The night of Feb. 10, 1958 will be remembered for the brilliant Aurora Borealis which occurred then. I first noticed it about 9 PM and thought at once of conflagration. When we looked from an open place, we saw a wide arch of flowing red which took up a third of the northern sky. It was brightest in the west, and was marked by upright beams of white. Beneath the red the sky was an intense green. Later the red color spread to the zenith, and into the east, though perhaps not so bright. Before dawn this morning the whole sky was red, and the late moon, almost down to the last quarter, shone as if in a misty sky. Only the brightest stars could be seen. *1958*

This was the fourth day of cold wind. The nights are below 10 degrees, the days cold and bright, the earth frozen all day. Glorious weather, if ever. It is a joy to cut wood on the sunny slopes. All other outside projects are suspended. The house is warm and cozy. I get up once during the night, keep up the fires in the fireplace and furnace. In the morning I start a good fire in the cookstove and keep it going as long as necessary. On the cold mornings a cardinal sings a few notes, and the titmouse. *1958*

I live with no care for the future, hardly for the present. Would it be better to foresee the inevitable and adjust my present life to it? Present conditions cannot endure, that is all we know for certain. Yet I live as if life would go on endlessly. But which way will it shift when it does change, and when will that be? *1961*

February 12 I withdraw from my customary occupations, woodcutting, picture framing, I cease to think of all the details so pressing on other days, and now it seems impossible that I will ever take them up again. *1961*

Our neighbors across the river greeted us as if we had been far away for a long time—it was 19 days since we had crossed the river. *1961*

I cut wood most of the short afternoon, working on the sunny hillside, so open now that every detail of the creek below was plain, the creek sparkled in the sun and ran with a sweet noise—if it could only run like this all summer. *1962*

Good writing should run freely like the brook, ever changing, full of surprises, yet a continuous stream. I wish I could write a book as freely as I write these lines—no careful construction, re-working or editing. It should come naturally as the melody of a bird. Only in this way can the imagination do its work. *1962*

Anna heard a towhee today. The stage is set for the phoebe. *1962*

My thoughts and activities turn toward the coming season, when woodcutting will require less time and I will begin garden preparations. That change will continue until woodcutting and tending fires are forgotten, and the garden will be of prime importance. I cannot conceive of it now. *1963*

We did the biweekly washing, which required 4 trips from the spring. I enjoy carrying the water, usually. One goes down the winding path to the lower bottom, across the level where the remains of last year's garden are still evident, through an open gate into Newt's old pasture. The path drops sharply down the bank to the spring. Dipping up the water from the flowing spring is always a pleasure, almost a rite, a spring is still a hallowed spot. The return begins with 10 or 12 giant steps cut in the soft bank, and crossing the bottom I always look north up the river toward Plowhandle Point with the riverbank cottonwoods cutting across. *1964*

February 13 Yesterday an expedition to Louisville. . . . An afternoon up and down the town—library, book store, art center, dreary business, mostly. A few live, real people met. . . . Louisville is a careless, shabby, friendly, easy going, ill-kept, makeshift, good-hearted place. Going to the city for us is like an expedition to an unfriendly mountain. *1954*

Moon got barely a horn over the ridge before daylight. *1961*

It seems that we attempt the labors of Hercules. Today it was canning meat, to save it from the warm air. I spent most of the morning cutting and trimming, Anna put it in jars, and her afternoon, her whole day was a busy one, for she baked bread, ironed and made yogurt, besides the canning. In the afternoon,

I cleaned and cut up the broken bones, etc., also worked on the hide. The goats and kids were all out together most of the day, they must have had a pleasant time. *1962*

A wet snow falling in the darkness, dripping from branches like rain, almost, for one knows it is not rain from the sound. I am up before daybreak, urged by that never-satisfied desire to "get things done," not just the daily chores but that which I do when the chores are out of the way. This gives zest to living, courage to meet the darkness and cold. *1964*

A bright, sharp day after yesterday's blow—this day was without any wind. . . . The evening was especially fine. As I went about my chores, the rays of the setting sun reddened the crest of the eastern ridge, a sway-backed horizon over which a bright-shining moon soon rose. Best of all was the voice of the creek coming up from the hollow, a composite voice made up of several, the variations of water running over stones. The western sky and the river were so bright one could hardly look that way, but there were the range of hills and well-known trees standing forth against the light. *1965*

The writing of the afternoon is still on my mind. It was about our building this house and first living in it. That was twelve winters ago. What induced us to come to this out-of-the-way place?—to build such a small simple house, scorning the conventional, and scorning the conveniences of modern living, scorning the division of labor by which everyone lives and makes life easy and luxurious, scorning money, having little use or respect for it, at least, working hard at what would be called tiresome drudgery nowadays, producing so much of our food, all our fuel. Yet we depend on the system developed by society to care for itself. We buy all our clothes ready-made, for instance, buy oil for lamps, etc. I think I can figure out why I came here, and what it means to me, but as for Anna—my reasons do not apply. Yet she is happy here, in her way, is averse to going to town, or to call on friends.

I wonder, too, what changes have taken place since our coming here. Nothing has happened to Payne Hollow to make it different than it was, except our coming; no road, no new building, no neighbors. Even across the river all is about the same, not a new house, only a new white fence. In general, two new trends are evident—the moving of city people to the riverbank, living for the summer in camps and trailers, and the great increase in outboards on the river. Yet these are only summer activities. . . . Much is the same that might have been changed. Wood is still our fuel, cut by hand, hauled in wheelbarrow. Kerosene lamps furnish our light, garden is even more extensive, my painting and writing go on about the same, and so does our music. . . . There is no use planning for the future. If it comes about that I am unable to keep on as in the past and present we can make the necessary adjustments when the time comes. Perhaps they will be made for me, naturally. *1965*

February 14 We launched the johnboat. Floats well, on top of the water. Rows well, too, though it is strange at first, so wide and high sided compared with the old one. After a short trial run together, I rowed across the river, against a stiff west wind. . . . Crossing the river I was struck by a fine view downstream, especially at that time, when the distant hills were dark under a sky breaking with light. *1953*

In the afternoon to Hanover, calling on, meeting and talking to quite a large number of people. I respect and admire them, have cordial feelings of friendship toward them. It distresses me that I cannot talk freely or express myself better. On returning I wince to recall my awkwardness. I did not say what I meant, perhaps because I did not know clearly or perhaps they did not care enough. At any rate I have given a false impression of my ideas. *1961*

A sudden, violent wind from the west in the night, then it stopped. More wind off and on, but not so strong, and today was cooler, with heavy slow-moving clouds, no sun, a light downstream wind. . . . Perhaps the dreary day helped, but as I pushed my wheelbarrow, the distant blue hills, the ranks of bare trees, the slow march of the huge clouds piled close—all this made it a beautiful day. *1962*

On the surface life goes on, people live together or meet casually, behaving like the normal, rational creatures they are supposed to be, but under the surface there is a raging furnace in each one, or a cold, frozen hell of despair. A truly brave cheerful man, with living faith and hope, is rare to see. But it is not easy to have faith and hope. A man is beset by awful dangers, ever on the point of breaking up and going under, to say nothing of the aggravations and miseries attendant on this system of living. How do men face all this who have not a love of beauty, who cannot derive peace and encouragement from this lovely earth or from the arts? *1962*

February 15 It is exciting business, unbelievable, a garden is, thinking of it now. *1963*

February 16 Yesterday evening we went to Jeffersonville to hear the Berkshire Quartet from Indiana University and it was quite worthwhile. Still daylight when outbound but light rain was falling on the return. On the highway when dashing through the night, meeting the glare of oncoming cars, the exaggerated sound of the wind and rain, the elements seem fierce and hostile. But on the riverbank in the hazy, diffused moonlight, with a gentle drizzle, looking out over the smooth, silent river, one feels that the earth is comforting and serene. *1962*

February 17 Spring is creeping in, while our minds are still wintry. The narrow dock puts forth green shoots, tiny green plants appear on the barren floor of the woods, the buds of the maples by the creek are red and swelling. Grass on protected slopes is a fresh green and the cover crops make a bright show in the landscape. *1954*

Today we ferried 20 framed pictures across the river and hung them in the store of Charles Hammack. All river pictures, all but 2 I think of steamboats, some painted 20 years ago. The lighting in the store is good, one wall brown, one red, one green. The pictures are hung above the shelves of groceries and above the long meat counter. *1957*

It is strange that painting is the last thing I get around to. All other activities must be brought up to date first. Perhaps at heart I am not a painter. But what else? I am always painting in my mind. Now as a tow of barges goes by on the still river, breaking the dark reflection of the hills with long lines of light, I see the pale tints of the sky past sunset reflected in the ruffled water. In the east a warm hazy moon, full or next thing to it. Painting is not a relaxation. It is a struggle, something we must rise to. *1962*

February 18 I was up very early, and Anna soon after. A long busy day, yet we played Brahms and Bach for an hour. We read some Thoreau after breakfast, and Proust after dinner. *1953*

This was a zero morning, the wind blows hard from NW, the river is so full of ice that we could not cross. Ice first appeared on Sunday after a very cold night, and it has increased until now the river is often nearly filled with great sheets, some snow covered, some so transparent it might be water, except that it is not ruffled by the wind. Then the ice floats on and open water appears, perhaps from shore to shore, except for the shore ice which is heavy on this side, especially at the bar. . . . The ice makes a terrible crashing sound when the edge of a floe grinds against the ice at the bar, where it piles up in broken pieces. The flow from the spring turns downstream on reaching the shore, making a shallow open cove, which I found to be full of shad. So we will feast on fresh fish, as will the dogs. *1958*

Still misty and wet, mild, the showers are not heavy. I enjoy it, body and spirit, it is soothing and peaceful. *1961*

Are the maple buds reddening? I see shoots and sprouts. Yesterday one peeper chirped down by the creek. This mild evening the far side of the river is ringing with them. Up the hill for mail this afternoon, and dug some sassafras root. Rain ceased at noon, after some hard showers. A clear evening, a new moon and Venus very bright. . . . This earthly life has been called a trouble and sorrow by many. But I have known no trouble or sorrow, nothing that went deep. And I cannot conceive of any. *1961*

Storage racks for my pictures. Thus it will be easier to show them to the curious than when I had to climb a ladder, hand them down from overhead, put them back myself. Not that I like to show them under any circumstances. It is agony to have strangers look at them. I can't even imagine how it would be to have them seen by someone who saw in them what I see. *1961*

No woodcutting today, and I miss it. It would be good to spend a winter just cutting wood, burning it to keep warm, cooking food and eating it, sleeping through the long winter nights. Then there would be time to watch the sunrise, and sunset, the stars and the moon, the winter birds and bare trees. *1963*

In the afternoon I went wooding up the river, working against the swift current, in backwater, around clogged drift and trees standing in water, the brown current rippling swiftly around the trunks and through the branches of a cottonwood, whose pointed golden buds were swelling. . . . When I landed in a little cove against the steep, forested bank and stepped ashore, it was virgin territory and I happily cut here and there, exploring, not knowing what I might find, so different from the worn hillside where I usually cut wood, among scattered trees every one of which is known and calculated by me, having been seen so often. Here too the leaves were thick underfoot, fallen branches scattered about. I loaded both ends of the boat, mostly with dry locust poles, worked out through the interlaced branches into the open river, whose current bore me and my load and the oak plank I was towing swiftly down to our landing. *1966*

February 19 I bought a new pocket knife last week, an event in my life. *1954*

This morning discovered that Daisy had a kid, not a surprise by any means. Later found another one in the stall with Betsy, an earlier one of Daisy's who had slipped between the palings. So the milking and feeding is on again. This year I had but a scant respite from milking; did not miss a day the past year, except for this week. *1959*

From our window we look down on the johnboat floating in the backwater, tied to the fence, a patient, loved member of our estate. Just now it is very handsome, its dark, solid, well-proportioned shape, with its dark reflection, on the bright water lighted by the low sun before us. *1959*

February 20 Today in midafternoon the ice broke loose with a loud roar. It seemed to start at about the narrows above us, and a strip perhaps 1/4 the width of the river, on this side of the center, came charging down into the motionless ice. The strip widened to both shores and now at twilight all is moving silently. *1958*

The important letter to mail was a refusal of Mrs. [Mary] Bingham's invitation to spent the weekend at her house in Louisville. No doubt it was truly cordial and well meant, but it would have meant considerable trouble for us, and I doubt if we could have contributed much to whatever gathering it might have been. For myself, I feel out of place with such people, I feel that my manners and my clothes are not right, I have little to say to them and express myself poorly, I seldom can be myself or get into my stride, I am usually quite miserable and wish I were somewhere else. Yet they are kindly people, just like the country people or Hanover people with whom we are on good terms, with whom we are easy and relaxed, as much as that is possible. *1962*

What friend is there who can be depended on? When with one I turn to another, and find that he, too, is not the one I seek. Yet all are good and kindly, even the young garage keeper of yesterday, and when he talked to me about his dog, I felt close to him. Yet on the surface I am repelled by most everyone. Contemporary life has no appeal, it is sterile and ugly, people are so, too, except in rare cases. *1962*

February 21 Some of the Madison stores are well known to us by this time, as we are to the store people. After trying all the hardware stores, Bierck's is our first choice. Its stock is not extensive; so we often go to Copeland's, a farmers' store, plain as the back porch of a farmhouse. Bierck's is neat and well arranged, it has an air of elegance and taste. The harness shop in the rear gives it color. The City Meat Market, names of proprietors unknown to us, has the dignity and reserve of a bank; or one might say, its peace and quiet are almost churchly. We go there once in a while, because it is the most likely place to get bones for the dogs. Our purchases of meat are very small, yet we are waited on with respect and appreciation. *1953*

My paintings are never seen in the best light, or by the right person. *1954*

One thinks—if he only knew what lay before him, how long he would live? It makes no difference. Act as though you were to live forever. No one knows the term of his life. *1961*

The flower buds on the elms are swelling, the soft maples by the creek are more red. Out in the johnboat I noticed the golden buds of the cottonwoods, in a tree whose branches were swept by the current. For some time there have been tiny green plants coming through the bed of leaves on the south hillsides. Spring creeps up on us unawares. *1966*

Up for mail this afternoon. Listened to the buzzing of bees within the hive. What faith and strength of purpose they have! *1966*

February 22 Some good painting in the afternoon. What a satisfaction to work intelligently. *1964*

February 23 Above all in the artist is his desire to express that portion of truth he has conceived; to put into words, tones or colors and shapes, his love and wonder and faith. All art is fundamentally religious. In painting, I am concerned with two aspects—one is a representation of what I see, working in three dimensions, in light and air, molding with my hands almost, a bit of the earth's surface. The other is abstract, a pattern of color and line, whose relation to the pictorial I am not sure of. Above these two, making a trinity, is the guiding force; in me, perhaps, a love of what I see and what I feel when observing the landscape. *1953*

Yesterday evening was open house at Classic Hall, Hanover College. Perhaps 75 people, mostly women, came to see our exhibition of painting. Coffee was served, with home-made cookies by ladies of the faculty. . . . Much talking and everyone seemed to enjoy themselves. Particularly the college ladies, who were like farmwives at a church supper. Many congratulations for me, some strange comments and blank gazing at the pictures, considerable intelligent appreciation. Certain pictures pleased many—the packet, the shantyboats, and the blue-shadowed Indiana hills, recently done, and without pictorial interest, unlike the other two just mentioned. It is good for me to see these pictures in another light and through other eyes. We returned late, a quiet, starry crossing, moon just rising. *1954*

February 24 Out on the river again. On shore, or even at the water's edge, the river is not fully absorbed. Once off shore in a boat it is a different world. *1953*

Another mild day, dispiriting somewhat, after the struggle of winter. With the cessation of cold I stop cutting firewood. The daily sawing and chopping are only a memory, yet the cold will return, and the woodcutting. *1961*

February 25 A visitor at dinner time, Boof Dolby. He came down the back way and strangely, the dogs barked little. He is a man whom dogs understand. An understanding mind he has, too. He made shrewd comments; remarked that our floor and window sash cost as much as all the rest of the "shack"; said our fireplace would throw out more heat if the back sloped inward, which is true. Dolby lives on Corn Creek, way up the hollow. He walked from there to Trout Bottom, here along the bench of the hill, and headed for home, over the hills. He arrived while we were eating, and had dinner with us. Boiled shad, blackeye peas, tomatoes, which he did not touch, and custard. He looked at the tea, asked if we had made any of sassafras. He uses for this the whole root, not just the bark. *1953*

Yesterday a burst of frog music, surely the voice of spring. *1957*

We went to Louisville for a concert, leaving about 6 PM, returning about midnight, crossing with the outboard through light drift on this side. Many times have we made such a trip, and I still leave with some apprehension and arrive home with relief. The fading daylight lasted about half way, we reached the city after it was lighted and traffic was heavy. The music is a joy, but through it I have thoughts of the weather (is it snowing?) and about the boat, perhaps (did I moor it high enough to be out of the reach of 6 hours' rise?). The drive home can be arduous, through the city and out into the blackness which is shot through by powerful beams of light. The heavy trucks overhaul us and roll past. Anna gets out some "pemmican"—peanuts, soybeans, raisins—and feeds me some as I drive. We seem to fly through the night, but all cars and trucks are going faster than we are. The bleakness of the plants at Charlestown. If the smoke streams away to the south I know it will be colder. What if the engine should stop and refuse to run, what if two tires were to go flat, as they did the other day? To get help might be difficult. What reception would I get if I knocked at the door of one of the lighted houses? At length the lights of New Washington appear, then soon we turn off the highway toward the river. The car is warm now. The end of the trip is reached, we get out into the cold night—but how comforting and quiet it is. The weather is seldom disagreeable, the crossing has always been easy, the dogs welcome us, we build a fire and get into bed. Another trip has been made. *1962*

Anna asked me why I write daily (almost). I can give no excuse. The reasons are subconscious. I am not writing for others to read and yet I enjoy writing and this is all of it I do now. I am deeply concerned with how each day, each minute is spent, and this is a kind of memorial to the passing days. *1962*

A chill day, the ground snow-covered early. . . . Woodcutting chores and painting. Just a little solid, creative painting and the day is good. It brings one close to the earth, makes the present moment exhilarating, the future hopeful; even though the painting is of a distant time and season and place. *1963*

February 26 Signs of spring—the cowbell across and down the river, the same one heard in summer evenings last year, now heard at the same hour. The flowering of the elms is now distinctly seen, the most exciting color of the year, like a deep, dull, portentous sound. *1954*

The life of an artist, even of such a one as myself, is an undercurrent which seldom shows on the surface. The crises, disappointments, ecstasy are not known even to the most intimate companion. Yesterday I completed a painting which makes me happier than anything I've done for years. It may be the beginning of a new era, of work on a new level. Yet, when I look at it again later on, its significance may have vanished. *1959*

I have much work to do now in preparation for the garden.

My hopes are at their highest, and the long toil over the spring summer and fall most pleasant to look forward to. *1959*

February 27 When I walked through the pasture on top of the hill this morning the song of the first field sparrow came through the mild air. We heard mockingbirds singing last week. I break ground in the garden, working the soil deep. *1954*

February 28 The morning was cloudy, without snow or rain, and the sun came out at midday. In the afternoon the wind blew very strong down the river, with clouds and waves of snow. The evening is clear, wind abated. It is worth getting out on the river on a February night, just as an adventure. There was not a breeze, none even down the hollow, to disturb the reflected hills which were all gray and soft in the diffused moonlight. This light slowly faded as the moon (just one night past full?) sank lower and the clouds became thicker. Then, imperceptibly, daylight began to penetrate, and for a long time the balance between light and dark was unchanged. Then it became lighter, with the hard fixed light of coming day. *1964*

www.ingramcontent.com/pod-product-compliance
Lightning Source LLC
Chambersburg PA
CBHW030928180526
45163CB00002B/499

* 9 7 8 0 8 1 3 1 9 3 2 5 0 *